PERFECT PHRASES™

for

VIRTUAL TEAMWORK

**Hundreds of Ready-to-Use Phrases
for Fostering Collaboration at a Distance**

Meryl Runion with Lynda McDermott

New York   Chicago   San Francisco   Lisbon   London   Madrid   Mexico City
Milan   New Delhi   San Juan   Seoul   Singapore   Sydney   Toronto

The **McGraw·Hill** Companies

1 2 3 4 5 6 7 8 9 10   QFR/QFR   1 7 6 5 4 3 2

ISBN   978-0-07-178384-2
MHID   0-07-178384-9

e-ISBN   978-0-07-178385-9
e-MHID   0-07-178385-7

McGraw-Hill books are available at special quantity discounts to use as premiums and sales promotions or for use in corporate training programs. To contact a representative, please e-mail us at bulksales@mcgraw-hill.com.

This book is printed on acid-free paper.

Contents

Foreword:
The Most Important
Person on the Team

Years ago, during a time when I was struggling to manage a dysfunctional team at work, my wife and I took our children to the circus. In one of the circus acts four acrobats balanced on a high wire, while three stood on their shoulders, two atop them, and finally one woman balanced at the very top of the remarkable human pyramid. They maintained their balance in this fragile formation as they walked the length of the wire.

I showed a photo of that performance to my team and asked my quarrelsome team members, "Who is the most important member of the team shown in this photo?" One noted that the woman has the most vulnerable position, another noted the strength of the acrobats forming the base of the pyramid, and still another noted that the second tier requires strength and particular balance. Finally they came to the unmistakable conclusion that each person's role is essential to the team performance.

We are each driven by three psychological needs: *autonomy*—our need to decide for ourselves, *competency*—our need to succeed at appropriate challenges, and *relatedness*—our need to care for others and have others care about us. When we work alone, we exercise our autonomy and increase our individual competency. The challenge of a team is to balance autonomy with relatedness. We need to make the leap to interdependent forms of the three needs: autonomy—the *team* decides, competency—*together* we can succeed at much greater challenges, and relatedness—we learn *from* and *accommodate* others as we work to influence others and ensure everyone on the team succeeds.

Being a member of a team that clicks and pulls off a significant and difficult task is a powerful, satisfying, and memorable experience. Teams that don't click are a drag. This book provides insights and phrases that can help ensure your team forms quickly, establishes meaningful goals, and fully engages everyone in meeting those goals.

While your ego is shouting, "Be reasonable, do it my way," I hope your intellect is open to the possibility that involving more people can increase the inspiration, energy, experience, creativity, resources, viewpoints, and scrutiny for accomplishing the task at hand. This book provides the tools, techniques, and actual phrases that can open egos to the marvel of teamwork.

Virtual is our new normal. I visit my infant granddaughter using FaceTime video conferencing. My only contact with Meryl is e-contact. Applying the skills in this book can help make your virtual teams as vibrant and effective as the most cohesive face-to-face team.

Good luck as you make the leap to teamwork.

Leland Beaumont
emotionalcompetency.org

Acknowledgments

When I start a project, I never know who might appear to make what kind of priceless contribution. Informal contributors virtually always show up in surprising creative ways, just when I need them. My thanks for this project go first to my virtual friend and colleague, Leland Beaumont, whose extensive experience in effectively leading high-powered teams helped guide the phrases on these pages. His input was consistently insightful and relevant, and often laugh-out-loud funny.

My second shout-out goes to Diane Windingland, whose critical eye helped me see where my voice became rigid and needed to loosen and lighten up a bit.

Thanks to Angela Thompson, whose unwavering support helped me through challenges that threatened to take me down and out. Everyone should have an Angela in his or her life—someone who sees your best and brightest and inspires you to rise to the courage of your convictions.

Annette Marquis offered valuable input on technology while in the middle of a Hurricane Irene blackout. Bev Kelley gave concrete examples of how virtual teams operate in educational institutions. Evan Hodkins helped me find the soul of virtual teams. Many generously shared their virtual communities and information exchanges with me and answered questions about how virtual teamwork happens, doesn't happen, and how they'd like it to happen in their industries and organizations.

Creating this book has been transformative, and I was blessed by an entourage of superstars who walked alongside me. I am grateful to each and every person who contributed virtually and otherwise.

Introduction

Welcome to a Virtual World, Where People Collaborate from a Distance

Guess who's surviving and thriving in the competitive global economy? The individuals and organizations that use virtual teamwork and virtual collaboration to their full potential. If you merely tolerate virtual teamwork as a necessary evil, you don't qualify. Today's thrivers embrace the value-added benefits of virtual teamwork, not just the cost-cutting benefits. They're juiced by the possibilities virtual collaboration offers and leverage online collaboration opportunities.

Even if virtual teams and virtual teamwork have been forced on you, you still have a choice. You can go kicking and screaming. You can try to manage virtual teams and off-site employees in the same way that worked (or didn't work) with your face-to-face or collocated teams. You can conduct business with virtual colleagues by passive-aggressively resisting the call to get on board with tools and systems that others leverage. You can go moping and griping and drag down momentum and spoil the fun and effectiveness for the rest of us.

Or you can shift your attention to the new dynamics of virtual collaboration and flourish. It's your call. If you're ready to make virtual teamwork a personal and organizational competitive advantage, or if you're already on board and need phrases to help, this book is for you.

There's a whole world of explosive collaboration out there that many professionals don't even know exists—even many who already work virtually. While some struggle to be heard by those higher up their organizational ladders, others post ideas on the team or company network with answers to questions and solutions to problems that get pushed up to the top tier because of their relevance. While some of us think we've stepped into the times by cooperating with colleagues and team members on projects, others have advanced cooperation to the level of collaboration that evolves at the speed of social dynamism—virtually instantly. While some of us wade through storehouses of data to get a single answer to a question—only to discover that the information is dated, others enjoy knowledge libraries and information-sharing protocols that allow people to access the relevant information exactly when they need it. It's a new era of pull communication where authority is earned through participation beyond credentials.

Welcome to the world of virtual teams today. We've simplified it for you to present its essence. We took the process into the very actionable format of the conversations you're likely to have during your journey. And believe us—that took some translating. Many resources describe what it takes to have successful virtual teams in general terms—but good luck figuring out what to do with that information when someone balks at embracing the collaborative applications that can exponentially increase your team effectiveness. We tell the story of how to speak from within the new paradigm of dynamic virtual teamwork and how to talk about the paradigm itself to those who haven't grasped the immensity of the change.

Virtual teams are not fads; they're today's reality and the future. Businesses boast successes that were impossible in a pre-virtual world. Professionals enjoy new levels of career success when they lead the way in virtual team excellence. We want your business and your career to experience the benefits too.

What's Virtual? Working Together...Apart

Virtual worlds, virtual teams, virtual work, virtual meetings, virtual assistants—virtual is the trend of our times. What does being "virtual" actually mean?

Virtual has the same roots as *virtue* and originally meant "effective because of certain inherent virtues or powers." Nice, huh? *Virtual* is also defined as "almost like." A virtual team is almost like a face-to-face team, except it operates in digital reality instead of physical reality.

One definition of virtual collaboration is:

People working interdependently on a common project across space, bridging organizational boundaries through webs of collaboration technologies

Despite the fact that the term *virtual* means simulated, virtual teamwork is very real.

Virtual teamwork is:

Work done by several associates with each doing a part but all subordinating personal prominence to the efficiency of the whole

Our working definition of a virtual team specifies mutual accountability. We define virtual teams as:

Work groups formed for specific purposes and held account-able for joint goals and shared deliverables

Virtual team members are interdependent in the way sports team members are interdependent. Team members don't work on everything together, but they are mutually accountable for results.

Working as a virtual team means working together apart.

Virtual Team Size Isn't Everything

If you work for a multinational global corporation, you probably think virtual teams are formal cross-functional units created for clearly defined projects that are officially chartered and sup-ported. (It's a mouthful.) These virtual teams deal with the fact that they aren't in the same physical space. They also may work in different time zones, speak different first languages, and be influenced by different cultures. And if the virtual team is an alli-ance, they may deal with different company cultures, too. Yikes!

If multinational global is not your world, your concept of a virtual team is scaled down. You may think of virtual teams as work groups that casually form at grassroots levels based on the pull of the work. That definition works too—if your group works toward a common result and members are accountable to each other. Ten years ago, when people spoke of virtual teams they meant the formal teams. Now they can mean either formal or casual groups, or a hybrid.

Either way, know that physical separation doesn't minimize the importance or legitimacy of the team or the power of digital collaboration. It does, however, affect the rigor with which you'll apply the team formation steps expressed in the phrases listed in the following chapters.

Team Members, Collaborators, Associates, and Allies

Surprise! You might be on a virtual team and not realize it! You also might have members on your virtual team who don't know they're members. Some members might think they're on a virtual team and in fact be an ally, an associate, a consultant, or a support person. One of the first formation steps a virtual team takes is to decide who is actually on the team. Here are some considerations:

1. They work toward a common result.
2. They have clearly defined roles and accountabilities.
3. They are essential to the effective functioning of the team.

Define the roles of all of your team members, and make sure members know them too. You don't want people discovering they're on the team at the performance review—or the postmortem!

Dynamic teams have lots of allies, associates, and support people whose input matters, but who aren't formal members. Identify those, too. You'll be returning favors with many of these people, but you won't hold them mutually accountable in the same way as members.

The Virtual Vehicle and Road Map—Two Essential Virtual Team Components

Okay. We like virtual collaboration and virtual teams. We see them as marvelously empowering. But we've seen and felt the pain that comes from dashing into them blindly. We've got that T-shirt. It reads, "I survived a virtual team disaster." This book is the way to avoid that.

Our goal is to help you thrive in your virtual team efforts. To support your success, we lay heavy emphasis on the virtual vehicle—the technology tools—and the virtual road map—the plan. As critical as these elements are, teams commonly minimize or dismiss them in favor of ineffective work-arounds and striking out unprepared. That means anyone tasked with the care and feeding of a virtual team is likely to require effective phrases to overcome resistance to the tools and planning that lead to success. Our experience and research identifies inadequate technology and planning as almost universal pain points, and the phrases here offer the remedies.

By the way, technology changes too quickly for us to be specific about our favorite software and apps here. You'll find recent information about collaborative technology preferences and downloadable forms for planning at www.speakstrong.com/teams.

How to Use This Book

We suggest you look through or even read this book sequentially first. Get a sense of what's in it—and what virtual team development involves. If you lead, sponsor, or are a member of a large and adaptive team (tasked with a creative mission), we recommend you apply each step of virtual team formation in detail. If you lead, sponsor, or are a member of a small and prescriptive team (with a set road map or procedure), consider the structure and steps of this book as recommendations and guidelines rather than rules.

Some of the phrases in this book are in a format for posting, e-mailing, and other methods of asynchronous or nonsimultaneous communication. Those are marked with a diamond symbol (❖).

Other phrases are written for synchronous or simultaneous communication. They are best used in real-time exchanges. Those are marked with the standard bullet (●).

We generally put the asynchronous phrases first because with virtual teams, asynchronous communication commonly comes first. For example, a team leader is likely to post or send out a meeting agenda (which members read at different times) prior to a meeting (where members interact simultaneously).

Once you're familiar with the available phrases, refer to the section that applies to your immediate needs and pick your phrases. Of course, you can adapt the phrases before you adopt and apply them for your needs.

Let's dive in!

PART I

PREPARATION

SECTION 1

Embrace Virtual Teamwork of Today

CHAPTER 1

Champion Virtual Team Potential

The first challenge of creating powerful virtual teams is to quickly get people to "get" this fact:

There is a social revolution and a business revolution going on, and virtual teams are on the cutting edge.

The way we did business before is over. Does your CEO understand that? Do your stakeholders understand that? Does the Board understand that? Does everyone who is or will become involved with the team understand we need to transform? That's the message of virtual teamwork. That's what is so important for everyone to realize before a virtual team or alliance even starts to take form. The social revolution is not just about consumers and entertainment. It's about enterprise. The virtual revolution is not just about relating as we once did through new media. It's about relating in all new ways. Virtual teams aren't just about being able to work across boundaries with new islands of cooperation. Virtual teams are about vast integrated webs of influence, generating and sharing ideas, collaborating instantly, having complete mobility, and forming dynamic partnerships as never before. It's not a minor change. It's a paradigm shift. And every time there's a new paradigm, it's time to reconfigure and reboot. Cut and start over. Embrace the whole dynamic new way of thinking about how virtual teams and alliances work and share the exciting news. The entire world (almost) has gone social—and mobile and virtual.

Perfect Phrases to Create a Dynamic Vision of Virtual Teams

As you can tell from the previous paragraph, there's a lot to be excited about with virtual teams. A clear vision motivates action. Use the following phrases to help you paint a picture of virtual teamwork possibilities that is so compelling that people won't just dabble. They'll be dazzled and dive in deep.

- ❖ Subject line: The Vision of Virtual Teams for (Organization Name, Project Idea, Etc.)
  - ❖ Most of us don't have a comprehensive idea of the dynamic power of virtual teams today. That's why I created a short (time, example: five-minute) presentation on how virtual teams can dynamize our (company, team, project, etc.). It's a (SlideShare/ YouTube video, etc.). Please click here (and enter this password: _____), enjoy, and post comments below. I invite you to pass it on.
- ● Virtual teams and virtual team technologies have evolved so much that instead of causing barriers, distance

managing actually leads to more collaboration and team-work than most collocated teams experience. It's like having all those experts in the same room.

- You wouldn't believe what people are doing on virtual teams these days! They share best practices at lightning speed and support each other on the ground where they are. They give people information they need when questions come up during client meetings or right as they reach impasses in their work. They have instant meetings and troubleshoot when problems arise, and they catch errors early on. They collaborate in small and targeted chunks just when input matters. They're really up to speed with business trends today.

- Virtual teams are about connection. They're cross functional, and that breaks down the hierarchy and distance silos. It's just not true anymore that people collaborate more in collocated teams. The fact is that if people are more than 50 feet away from each other in the same location, they don't collaborate much. Virtual teams have the team on their desktops, mobile apps, and phones. They carry the team around with them, and that's a lot closer than 50 feet.

- My experience with virtual teams is that we bounce ideas off each other a lot. There's a dynamic immediacy—a back-and-forth. That means projects move forward at a faster clip. Input happens at earlier stages, so we make changes and adapt sooner—which is extremely efficient when we need quick answers.

- One great thing about virtual teams is the capacity to update team members on the activities of the team as a whole without needing to be physically present. Members can address the group for input and ideas more readily.

● There's more flexibility in virtual teams. Because travel time means turning on your laptop or iPad and logging on wherever you are, it's easier for people to fit virtual meetings into their calendar. That means they can be available more readily.

● I've had fabulous experiences with virtual teams. For example, (give a brief example). We never could have accomplished (achievement) like that if we had limited ourselves to a headquarter location.

● If we go virtual in forming this team, we can create satellite teams in locations close to the customers. That will save costs and ensure our teams are aligned with the local culture.

● Companies that approach working virtually as a progressive and competitive strategy are more likely to survive and thrive in the coming decades. I want that to be us.

● Virtual teams provide us with options. We won't be limited by physical location from getting the right people on the team. That means people can be a part of projects they couldn't before. We won't need to compromise on our best talent.

● Virtual teams tend to get right to business when they meet virtually in ways they don't when face-to-face. I often find we get the same amount done in half the time.

CHAPTER 2

Evangelize Business Social and Collaborative Technology

If you want to paint a compelling picture of virtual team potential, you have to talk about collaborative software and teamwork tools. It's the tools that make this revolution possible. Some of the most effective and dynamic software and apps that increase efficiency and create a competitive edge are only a few years or even months old. To know what people are doing with social and collaborative technologies is to understand what virtual teams are capable of today. The people who are ahead of this curve can light the way by sharing how people can connect in new ways.

❖ Notice to (employees, associates, stakeholders, etc.): It's your conversation and your career.

   ❖ People are talking like never before. It's not just the social butterflies or the technophiles that are having the lights go on. Social networks, business chat feeds, and collaborative sharing tools open doors for us as an organization and for you in the job you do every day. Just in case you thought the tools don't matter, click here to see that yes, they really do. Watch the three-minute video and join the discussion we have started about how our thriving community of networked professionals is solving problems and creating new opportunities each day.

❖ Notice to (employees, associates, stakeholders):
  ❖ Here are a few of the ways people are using our online network to increase their productivity. They're following our top deals, collaborating online privately and securely, reducing e-mail traffic by posting to groups and discussions, uploading files to our knowledge library, and discovering experts who help them solve problems and close deals more quickly. We want you to join the conversation.
  ❖ How are you using our online network? Post to this discussion and share your wins and best practices.

● Virtual team tools are what make virtual teaming so dynamic. Well, actually it's the use of the tools, not the tools themselves.

● Collaborative software can more than make up for the lack of proximity. Once you've experienced the dynamic flow of instant access and easy idea sharing, anything else can seem static by comparison.

● People aren't just moving to (new technology, example: the cloud) because it's the latest and the greatest. They're doing it because it works and they're getting results. It enhances productivity exponentially.

● Here are some stats for you from Salesforce.com. Teams that use their networks effectively have 27 percent fewer meetings and a 30 percent reduction in e-mail. They have a 39 percent increase in collaboration and find information 52 percent faster than those who don't.

SECTION 2

Create a Strong Virtual Team Foundation

CHAPTER 3

Clarify the Business Need for a Virtual Team

Wow. We just told you how great virtual teams are, and now we suggest you might not need a virtual team at all. What's up with that? Well, not every situation calls for a team, and sometimes you can get what you need with a collocated team, an existing team, or working through standard processes. Too often, leaders and managers will try to force the need to fit a tool or approach rather than the other way around. These phrases will help you make sure you and your associates form a virtual team for the right reasons, if at all.

Tip and Warning!
Employ Every Team Formation Step

Every step is for you and your team in one form or another. Small, casual virtual teams and virtual alliances don't need the formal structures that are mandatory for larger, formal ones.

(continued)

Teams who work on predictable projects don't require as much team preparation and coordination as creative ones. That doesn't mean small or defined teams can skip the setup steps entirely. The temptation for a team of any size—from 2 to 200 members—can be to jump right into action without any pre-liminaries. *Can* it work? Sure. You might find you went in sharing the same assumptions. However, when it doesn't work, you'll long for an early retirement when, instead, you could make things happen virtually. Skipping the preliminaries is a recipe for confusion, misunderstandings, and failure. All teams need at least an informal version of each step.

Perfect Phrases to Clarify the Project Business Need

The beginning is the perfect time to clarify the business need that *might* lead to forming a virtual team. Clear purpose gives stakeholders the understanding they need to decide how to meet the need, and then if they elect to form a virtual team, it gives that team the information they need to create their charter, or team map. (Some teams use the term *charter* to mean purpose or mission. We use *charter* to refer to all aspects of defining and mapping a team, such as goals and norms, etc.) If you can't answer the questions in this section, you're not ready to form a team or take a next step.

❖ Notice to (stakeholders). We (created a new group and) opened a discussion about (the intranet, company business network, etc.) to clarify the business need of (challenge). The results of this discussion will guide our decisions about forming a team to address our challenges.

❖ Based on the comments in our business need discussion, we formulated the following business need statement.

❖ Please post comments and concerns before we finalize it and move on to discussing goals.

● What performance or business challenge do we need to meet?
  ● How can we state that more precisely and concisely?
● What's broken that we need to fix?
  ● How can we flip that statement into a positive?
● What is the primary client or customer need?
● What's the true north of this project? The guiding compass?
● Let's summarize what we have as clearly and succinctly as possible.
  ● Do those words light a fire in everyone's belly? Or do we need to keep talking?
● Is this description good enough for prime time? If, for example, you needed to create a compelling team charter based on this, plus explain to your boss that this is a priority, would this give you what you need?
● How does the purpose align with and support the organizational mission?
● Is that as clear as we can make it? Would that purpose set a team up for success with a clear mandate from the outset?
● Let's fill in the blank. We need to _____ because _____.

- Can we present an elevator pitch now? Would the pitch be compelling and effective in recruiting members?

- If the project had a bumper sticker, what would it say?

- Have you thought about why you (we) really need this team?

- Have you identified and talked to the key stakeholders who have a vested interest in the results? What do they say they want?

- Why would the key stakeholders want and support this team?

- What's the point? We're not talking objectives here—this is the big picture of what the team is about. Why do we need to accomplish our mission? Not *want*, but *need*.

Perfect Phrases to Determine If a Virtual Team Is the Best Way to Go

These phrases and questions challenge the assumption that you need a team at all, and they reveal what options best serve the purpose. If you do form a virtual team, do it for the right reasons.

❖ Notice to stakeholders: You'll find a survey on our shared workspace eliciting input regarding the best structure to address the (business mission from previous step). Please complete it within (time frame).

   ❖ Based on the discussion/survey results, we've decided to form a virtual team to accomplish (purpose). Please watch for further communication for goal input.

We have our purpose. Let's list all possible options for accomplishing this purpose.

Is there another way to meet that purpose that might be more efficient and effective than forming a team?

Can we get the expertise we need in one location, or do we need multiple locations?

Why do we need to create a team to accomplish this? Why is a team the best approach? Let's not just say "form a team" and declare our work accomplished.

Why a virtual team? What in particular about this purpose suggests a virtual team is the best way to achieve it?
- What could a collocated team do that we couldn't easily replicate in a virtual team?
- Is that essential? Do the benefits of a virtual team outweigh the limits?

● What aspects of virtual teamwork do we want to be sure to take advantage of in this process?
  - Are we willing to invest in the applications and training to be able to leverage those advantages?

● Fill this in. We're addressing the business challenge of (purpose statement) by forming a team because (reason). We are forming a virtual team instead of a collocated team because (reason).

Why *this* team?

Let's clearly state why this virtual team is important to the organization.

CHAPTER 4

Create Preliminary Goals

I t's too early for defined goals, but right after you clarify team purpose is the perfect time to identify generally what you want this team to do. A word of caution: avoid locking the team into rigid subgoals that might not be the strongest or most useful for the on-the-ground reality. It's best if the virtual team sets its own team goals.

While a clearly stated mission (such as putting a man on the moon and bringing him home) provides important direction, at this stage, preliminary goals and subgoals are best as guidelines or a draft.

Perfect Phrases to Ask Stakeholders to Identify Preliminary Team Goals

Preliminary goals provide a launching point for the people who are actually tasked with the outcome to clearly state the goals in ways that create goal identity. You'll find more on goals in the launch section. Use the words "draft" and "preliminary goals" to keep early goals nonbinding.

- ❖ Notice to stakeholders: We started a discussion in our group to identify team goals. Goals are endpoints and indicate what we want the team to deliver. Please join the discussion and share your needs and requirements. The discussion asks, when all is said and done, how would you decide the team was successful?
  - ❖ Based on the discussion, we formulated recommended preliminary goals. Please complete the survey at (location).
  - ❖ Based on the survey, we have set the following preliminary goals.
- Now that we know why we're forming the team, let's get clearer about what we expect it to deliver. Let's fill in the blank. We expect this team to deliver...
- Just what is the team supposed to accomplish?
- Let's keep the terms broad here to give the team room to set their own goals and objectives.
- Our role is to give the team enough information about the purpose and team deliverables for them to be able to create a compelling charter with goals and subgoals they can translate into objectives.
  - Do we need to rough out some of the subgoals and timelines, or will the team be better able to do that?
- I get why we're doing it. Help me paint a picture of exactly what the deliverables will be.

- Okay, I know it's impossible to know exactly what the end product will be until we get into it, but let's pretend we can. What does it look like? How will we know we've made it?
- Why do we need just that?
- Does that definition allow enough room for the team to put their name on it?

- Let's each describe the preliminary goals to the best of our understanding to make sure we're on the same page.

- Is that the best way to state the preliminary goal? Let's play devil's advocate. Imagine it's (end time). Imagine we've gotten what we asked for, but it's not what we thought we were asking for. You know the saying: "Be careful what you ask for, you might get it." So if the team achieved the goal as stated, would you be satisfied? Why?
  - Let's each describe a possible scenario where a team delivers according to the goals set here but it doesn't match our expectations.
  - How could we keep that from happening?

- We're asking our team to strive to new levels to achieve these goals. The goals need to be worth the sacrifice. That means attainable and yet a stretch. Are we there?

- Are these goals worth getting home late for dinner?

Perfect Phrases to Quantify Stakeholder Expectations

How are you going to track all that? Have each stakeholder put his or her desires into measurable outcomes.

- Let's talk metrics. What are you looking for? What is the dashboard that you'll go to every day to know how the team is doing?
- We want our dashboard to match what you look at. Our metrics need to be visible so people can know what is being measured and monitored, and team results meet your expectations.
- A year from now, what would it take for you to recommend that this team continue working together?
- What do you want or need from this team that you haven't been able to get in another way?
- What added value do you expect to see from this team and its work?

CHAPTER 5

Get the Right People on the Team

D on't skip over this step! Someone with distinguished experience might be a virtual team nightmare. Virtual teamwork isn't for everyone. If you hire the wrong people, you might be stalled arguing over simple collaboration tools or over the importance of putting team interests ahead of their own instead of using the tools to create great results.

Interviewing for professional expertise for virtual teams is similar to interviewing for in-house promotions or job changes. For phrases for in-house interviews, see *Perfect Phrases for Managers and Supervisors* (Runion, McGraw-Hill, 2010). We focus here on competencies and interviewing for virtual dream team skills.

Perfect Phrases to Identify Needed Competencies

What skills will you need on your virtual team? Virtual teams aren't for everyone. Some people who play well with others face-to-face don't play well on virtual teams. Make sure your team has collaborative skills as well as industry skills.

❖ (Post to company social/business network.) I'm tasked with identifying the competencies we need for our team to (purpose). What competencies would you select for? What warnings or advice do you have for me?

❖ Notice to stakeholders: Competencies for (name) team:
  ❖ Our preliminary list of competencies is listed on the team wiki at (location). You are invited to add to the list.
  ❖ We have finalized the list of our competencies. You'll find them posted on the team site at (location).

● Who do we need on the team? Let's start with the core and branch out.

● What skills are essential for this project? Let's start at the core and branch out.

● How can we interview and assess team candidates for adaptability and collaborative skill?

● Complete this team formation statement: We're forming this team to achieve (goal), and deliver (specific outputs) to (client or customer) by (deadline) to solve (problem). To accomplish that, we need these competencies.

● Who here has had a great virtual team experience? What competencies made it work?
  ● Did you recruit for that ability, or did you just get lucky?
  ● How did you or could we word that when we interview for that skill?

- Who here has had a disappointing virtual team experience? What caused it to fail?
  - How could we word that in our list of competencies?

- Let's start with the competencies we require of all team members. And since we're working remotely, let's start with collaborative technology skills. What types of collaborative tools do we need members to be able to use?
  - How proficient do we need them to be in each?
  - Are we open to candidates who aren't familiar with some of those tools but who are interested in learning?
  - Does lack of familiarity with any of these tools serve as a red-flag indicator that a person might lack other skills or experiences we need? For example, if someone is inexperienced with Excel, can we assume he or she doesn't have the administrative skills we need?
  - What software and applications do we use every day that we consider basic for any team member?
    → Should we require existing skill, or is willingness to learn acceptable?
    → Think of a time when you've been surprised by someone's lack of skill with software, applications, and other business tools. What happened? How can we translate these experiences into stated competencies?

- Are any of the skills on our list outdated? How can we know that our list isn't regressive? I see we don't have the ability to save things to floppies on the list—but that doesn't mean we're current.

- Who do we need to talk to in order to really be able to get this list updated and relevant?
- Would the people actually doing the work agree with this list?
- Are there some things on the list that are more essential for some team roles than for others, or are they required for all?

- Let's look at communication skills. We can start with the kind of skills everyone needs and work into the ones unique to each role.
  - Have any of you ever had a team member who would have been great except he or she couldn't communicate well? What kind of challenges did you struggle with? What was lacking?
  - How can we flip those flaws into their opposites—into specific competencies we want to interview for?
  - We want the team to be inclusive, and we also need to have enough of a shared language to be able to succeed. How will we define competency in terms of language abilities? Should use of a translator be an option?

- Let's look at our dream team. From Bill Gates to the person who delivers your mail—imagine anyone we want is willing and available for this. Who would we pick, and why?
  - How do we translate that into competencies?

- Let's go over our projects and create a list of competencies for each. Then we can translate that into roles.

Perfect Phrases to Interview for Collaborative Virtual Communication Abilities

You've identified your competencies. Here are ways to interview for adaptiveness and collaborative ability indicators. How effectively do candidates use the tools and engage in virtual team communication? One way to demonstrate virtual team communication application abilities is by applying the tools your team will use in the selection process.

❖ We're staffing a dream team for (project). We're looking for expertise in (industry area).
  ❖ To apply, please respond by creating a short video or SlideShare explaining why you'd like to be a member of this dynamic team. Upload it to the following FTP site.
  ❖ To apply, please respond by filling out the online questionnaire located at (location).
  ❖ To apply, please create a simple audiovisual presentation that both discusses and demonstrates your ability to communicate virtually.

❖ Thanks for your application.
  ❖ The next step for our team candidates is to participate in the online discussion about (relevant topic), which you'll find at (location).
  ❖ The next step for our team candidates is to review the agenda for your virtual interview and make improvement recommendations directly to the document. That agenda is located at (location).

What do you like about working collaboratively?

What is your favorite collaborative tool?

- How do you use it?
- Why is it your favorite?
- What have you been able to accomplish with that tool that you couldn't have without it?

How do you handle e-mail when you work virtually? How do you use (have you used) social networks (the company community network) to increase your effectiveness?

What is your current experience level with cloud computing?

- How have you used cloud computing effectively in the past?

- Have you worked virtually before? Tell me about it.
  - What did you like about it?
  - What was your biggest challenge when you worked virtually?
  - How did you handle that challenge?

- How did you or would you handle an unresponsive virtual team member—for example, someone who doesn't post documents as promised?
  - How did that work for you?

Is there a virtual medium that you just don't like? Which? Why?

How would you or did you handle a team member that underused the technology?

- Was it effective?

Who do you see as responsible for the smooth functioning of a virtual team?

- Why?

- How have you stepped in and taken a leadership role in a team setting because the situation called for your skills?
- How have you stepped back because the situation called for someone else to take the lead?
- Describe your use of collaborative software and applications.
  - What programs do you use?
  - How have you customized your software and apps to your needs?
- How do you respond when you encounter a technological glitch?
  - Tell me about the last time you resolved one.
- How have you adapted to working with team members or associates in different time zones (on different shifts)?
  - What specific systems or processes have you found to be useful to keep different shifts or time zones aligned?
- What challenges have you experienced working with people from different cultures?
  - Share some examples of how you bridged cultural gaps in the past.
- How do you stay connected at airports, hotels, conference centers, and other places when you're traveling?
  - Does that give you full mobility? For example, can you edit documents at an airport?
- What do you do when you have a technological challenge on the road?

Perfect Phrases to Determine Suitability for Self-Directed and Off-Site Work

This section helps you weed out those who aren't suited for self-directed or off-site work.

- Describe how you manage your time when you work virtually.
- How is working virtually different from working proximately for you?
  - How do you adapt?
  - What do you do differently?
- If you were forming a virtual team for this project, what questions would you ask potential candidates?
- If you were forming a virtual team for this project, what qualities and competencies would you look for?
- What was the worst team experience you ever had?
  - What went wrong?
  - What did that experience teach you?
- Some people are more comfortable than others working independently, without face-to-face contact over long periods of time. How does that work environment, impact you?
- What do you need to know about this team to decide for yourself if it's a fit for you?
- How much social interaction do you need? Describe your perfect amount of social interaction in an average workday.
  - How do you meet your social needs when you work from home or independently?
- Do you have a dedicated work space?

Describe your virtual ideal workday.

Do you have any limitations that could interfere with your ability to do virtual work?

How do you build relationships virtually?

We're considering you for (team role). What competencies would you think we need in that role?

- How skilled are you in each of those areas?
- We also pinpointed the following competencies. (Identify competency the person omitted.) Do you consider that to be an important competency? Why or why not?
- Do you have that competency?

(Name), how many teams are you on right now?

- Would those commitments interfere with your ability to contribute to this team?

Do you have other commitments that would be a conflict of interest for being a member of this team?

- How would your other commitments limit or interfere with your being a part of this virtual team?

I'll get back to you as we decide who is on the team.

As I learn more about your skills, interests, and commitments, I don't believe this will be a good fit right now. Thanks for talking with me about it.

Perfect Phrases to Get the Inside Scoop About a Team Member Candidate

People might hesitate to warn you of a possible team member, but specific questions aimed at what kinds of structures draw out the excellence in someone are a different story. These phrases avoid the bad/good, yes/no false dichotomy traps that cause people to tread lightly in sharing their opinions about a potential virtual team member.

The best virtual team candidates might be less visible than company superstars who make a name for themselves. If you look behind and around the big names, you might discover the wind beneath their wings—or those people whose supportive contributions actually drove their success.

- I know (name) is an amazing (example: marketing expert). I'm wondering if a virtual team situation would be a fit for her or if she shines the most in a face-to-face situation. What are your thoughts?
  - What challenges might (name) have contributing to this virtual team?
  - How do you think she would contribute?

- Do you think (name) thrives on autonomy and working independently, or might he flourish in a team setting—particularly a virtual team setting?

- (Name) is a brilliant thinker and idea generator. I wonder how she might work on a virtual team where sometimes the team will want to take things in a different direction and the best choice for the team interests is to let go. Thoughts?

- I know you managed (name) for a while. If you were considering him for an assignment on a virtual team, what kind of guidance would you provide to enable the best results?

- I don't want to set anyone up for failure, and virtual teams aren't for everyone. If you were considering (names) for (project), what concerns and considerations might you have?

● If we include (name) on our virtual team, what kind of training would you recommend prior to the team launch?

Perfect Phrases to Get Someone to Volunteer for the Team

Contributor Lee Beaumont shared how his manager got him to volunteer for teams by creating interest. This is a less direct approach. If you take it, don't manipulate or trick anyone into volunteering. Instead, fuel intrigue and interest in legitimate issues while you acknowledge genuine strengths of the hoped-for volunteer. Timing is an important aspect of skillful communication. Trickery isn't. Here are some phrases you can use.

● (Name), a crisis is looming. I'll tell you about it.

● (Respected person) and (other respected person) are working with me to form a team to address the issue.

● You're uniquely qualified to be a key contributor because (reasons).

   ● I knew you'd have some healthy skepticism that would help us define the issue.

   ● You're right about (concern). How would you address that if you were on the team?

   ● What other obstacles do you anticipate this team would face?

   ● Oh, wow. If anyone could address that obstacle, it would be you.

- I'd love to have you on the team. What would you say if I asked you?
- Thanks for volunteering! I was hoping you would.

Perfect Phrases to Invite or Assign Team Members

Employees may or may not welcome being the chosen one. Carrots are better than sticks when you assign team membership, but don't pretend you're using a carrot when you're really using a stick. These phrases invite or assign team membership in the best possible way. Refer to "Perfect Phrases to Create a Dynamic Vision of Virtual Teams" in Chapter 1 for help explaining the advantages of virtual teams.

- I want you on this virtual team because (reason).
- We're working toward an outcome, and we need your help. We need you on our virtual team.
- You've been chosen/selected/assigned to be a member of a new virtual team because of your skill/background in (area).
- You were selected for the team. It is an exciting project. And not only will you be able to contribute extensively—you'll learn a lot.
- Guess what. You're on the team. I understand this isn't something you signed up for, so let's talk about how we can make it work for everyone.
- Okay, you got put on team (name). No—we're not delusional. We know you're already beyond busy. We need you

on the team because (reason). Let's talk about what that means in terms of your overall commitment.

- I know it's a time constraint for you, and if I could have found someone else who is equally qualified, I would have. Because of your skills in (area), we need you on this team. We (have talked to/will talk to) your boss. Tell us your thoughts about how we can make it work.

- We selected you for (role) on (team) because (skills). I'll start with the benefits to you and then invite you to be frank about every concern. I also want to discuss what you need to make this assignment work with your existing commitments.

CHAPTER 6

Prepare for the Virtual Team Launch

The virtual team launch is the team road-mapping session. It sets a direction that can lead to success or failure.

Perfect Phrases to Clarify End Users and Their Goals

Stakeholders and end users might want different things. Identify end users and their needs to help the team finalize their goals.

- Let's define our end users. If there's not a benefit to them, they'll have a hard time adopting our final product, even if it's mandated by the senior leadership. Let's start listing the players.

- Let's give them names and traits and talk about what they want and don't want.

- What are their principal goals?
- What does success look like for each?
- How do the end user and stakeholder goals align?
- Where are they opposed?
- How can we align them?

Perfect Phrases to Invite Active Sponsors to Employ Best Practices

A team sponsor is usually one or more senior executives who strongly believe in the team mission and will provide cover and support if and when the team needs it. Sponsor support can make or break a team. Invite the sponsor to embrace sponsor best practices. These practices might include sending messages or even opening the team launch. You can find a sample "Virtual Team Sponsor Best Practices" list posted at www.speakstrong .com/teams.

- ❖ (Team name) stakeholder best practices:
    - ❖ To support the team in its success, we've compiled a list of stakeholder best practices. You can find it posted at (site).
    - ❖ To reinforce and coordinate your efforts, we invite you to comment on the post.
    - ❖ We particularly invite you to add best practices that have worked for you as a team sponsor in the past. Stories and details are welcome.
- What difference can active sponsors make in team success? It can be the difference between success and failure.

In fact, many researchers say the number one contributor to team success is active and visible sponsors. We invite all sponsors to actively take measures on a consistent basis to support the team efforts.

- Here are just a few best practices that team sponsors can employ to support the success of the team.
    - Actively review progress
    - Build support and enthusiasm for the change
    - Provide unwavering support throughout the process
    - Build a strong sponsor coalition for the team purpose and process
    - Model the change
    - Make sure managers relay a consistent message
    - Manage expectations of stakeholders and customers
    - Build awareness about the importance of the project

- As a sponsor, your support can make the difference between our success and failure. To be able to use your expertise and influence, I'd like to be able to ask you freely for help and input where I see it benefitting the team outcome. Are you open to that?

Perfect Phrases for Prelaunch Updates

During the interval between the team staffing and the launch, keep people informed and connected with considered updates. Prelaunch updates provide access to background information, particularly for team members who are less familiar with the project history or with other team members. Updates also keep the impending launch high in team members' awareness, address preliminary issues, notify team members of changes, and help prepare for the launch. (I refer to a stakeholder worksheet in the phrases. You'll find a link to a downloadable copy at www.speakstrong.com/teams.)

❖ Subject line: Welcome to (Team Name), Action Required
  ❖ Body: Hooray! The Team Launch Meeting is scheduled for (time, date). Please confirm by (date) as attendance is required of all members. Here's some prep for you—within the next week, please complete your team profile on the team site at (location). We want to know all about you as a member of our team!

❖ Subject line: (Team Name) Prereading for Team Launch, Action Required
  ❖ Body: Prereading for this Team Launch Meeting has been posted on the team site at (web location/shared folder). Please review the information to prepare for team launch discussions about the project, deliverables, and milestones. Also review the profiles of other team members and the leader to help us begin to get acquainted. See you at the launch meeting!

❖ (E-mail) Subject line: (Team Name) Prelaunch Activity
  ❖ Body: Please e-mail me a description of one of your hobbies before our next meeting. As an icebreaker, we'll share these descriptions and try to match them up with our new team members.

❖ We're planning for a great launch. It's your launch too. So keep in touch about what you need or recommend to make it a successful event.

❖ We created the shared folder at (web or file address) for team use. Product development updates have been posted to the team resource center to get you on board in preparation for the team launch. Review these items to prepare to make the most efficient use of everyone's time at the team launch.

    ❖ Special acknowledgment goes to (name), who (example: posted a SlideShare presentation to introduce team members to the purpose of this project). You'll find that at (location).

❖ One of the launch activities will be to identify and prepare to manage team stakeholders. Between now and the launch, please speak with individuals who will be impacted by your participation in the team to identify their concerns about your involvement. You'll find a worksheet to help you identify and manage stakeholders on the team site.

● For those new to (project field), please complete the tutorial on the team site regarding (example: cultural norms in the launch area).

PART **II**

LAUNCH

SECTION 3

Create a Road Map

The team creates the team charter or road map at the team launch. That map is vital to the success of the team. For formal chartered teams, a face-to-face launch is ideal. Less formal teams might opt out of a face-to-face, but they should have a virtual launch meeting at the very least. If your virtual team is more of an alliance or partnership, scale down the recommendations here, but don't ignore them. If your team is already launched, review this section anyway to see what elements in team formation you skipped over. You can use it for remedial cleanup work.

Face-to-face launches are commonly one to two days. Virtual events are best limited to two hours, so if you bypass a face-to-face, schedule long breaks or a series of shorter events to cover charter details in your virtual format.

The agreements you reach in the launch and early formation stages are intended to serve the team, not the other way around. If systems and protocol interfere with effectiveness, renegotiate them.

CHAPTER 7

Set Clear Direction

Where are you going? It's hard to create a map if you don't know. Start by getting your direction clear. You started this process in Chapter 3. Review the steps and results of that work as you prepare your team launch.

Perfect Phrases to Open a Launch Meeting and Introduce the Virtual Team Purpose

While relationship building is a critical component of your launch meeting, people want to know why the project matters and what the work is before they get to the softer relational stuff. Immediately provide the vision of the project and an understanding of why the mission is important. If necessary and possible, open with an explanation from top executives or key sponsors to underscore the significance of the team mission.

- Welcome! Because this project is critical to the success of the organization, (senior leader) will personally (digitally) present the information we need to be able to create our charter. She'll tell you exactly why we formed this team and what the team is expected to accomplish. Every person on this team was selected for a specific reason, and we each need to know why we and our teammates are essential to the team as a whole and to the organization.

● Welcome! I'll explain the purpose of the team, the importance of the team, and what is expected of team members in detail. This is important to the success of our team, so we'll go through it together to ensure that everyone clearly understands the individual and team accountabilities. Please speak up, ask your questions, and raise any issues, doubts, or reservations so we can address them. Let's begin.

● This is an exciting day. Right now, we're a group. By the end of the day (the next few days), we'll be a team.

● We've been tasked by (name/function) with an important project. As you know, our company mission is to (mission). To help us achieve that, we formed this team to (purpose). This is important because (reason).

● Necessity is the mother of invention. I know I'm not the only one who is bugged by the way we (complaint/problem/issue). Well, we get to do something about it. We have been asked to solve the problem of (challenge).

● I'm excited about the project because (reason).

● This project is important to our organization because (reason).

Perfect Phrases to Break the Virtual Ice and Introduce Team Members

Once your team members get the big picture of the team purpose, they're ready to meet the other team members. Give a quick overview of who's on the team, including the reason why they were selected. If some members were chosen by default because they were the only ones available or something similar, you can still refer to how you expect them to contribute to the team. Icebreakers set the team tone. The best icebreakers are ones that are closely tied to the desired purpose, performance, and excellence.

- A great thing about virtual teams is that we tend to get right to business. Before we do that today, let's break some virtual ice. It's time to introduce the team members.

- What a group we have! I'll start by introducing everyone and listing the skills that led to their selection to the team. Later, we'll introduce ourselves and add any additional skills I might have overlooked.

- Each team member was assigned a team buddy for a precall so you could introduce each other to the team. Let's go around alphabetically and introduce our partners.

- Let's each fill in the blanks,
    - Personal accomplishments that I'm proudest of are…
    - Professional accomplishments that I'm proudest of are…
    - Some unique skills and experiences I bring to this team are…
    - My expectations and hopes for this virtual team are…

- We've all been on teams of one sort or another. Let's go around and each share an example of a team we've been on that worked—our dream team—and what made it successful.
  - What have you heard that could be useful to us here?
  - What kind of metrics would reflect that kind of team?
- Here's a funny way to remember my name. (Some word association with your name.) Let's go around the team and give each other ways to remember our names.
- Let's go around and share our heroes and why they affect us so deeply. We'll go in reverse alphabetical order by last names.
- Let's each describe our favorite job and explain why we liked it.
- I asked you to e-mail me a description of one of your hobbies before the launch. Now I'll ask one of you to share the list, and we'll try to match the descriptions with our new team members.

Perfect Phrases to Introduce the Virtual Team Charter Process

Okay, the introductions are over. It's back to business. Now that the team has the overview of the purpose and a sense of who's on board, it's time to get into the charter details. The charter is the team road map. It's deep focus time.

- What great introductions! Now, I hope you refilled your coffee and sharpened your pencils. What we are about to do will set the direction of this team for the next (antici-pated duration of the project). This team has been given a mission to fulfill by senior leaders. They considered every word when they formulated what I read in the opening. We need to make it our own. We will put it in our own words today. We will go over every phrase down to the word until we completely grasp our mission and have an expression of it that inspires us.

- Some people think building a team purpose is meaning-less fluff. Some team missions are. It's up to us to create one that can serve as a touchstone to keep us focused. And trust me—you'll need to be able to clearly explain why this team is important to your managers and col-leagues. If you're not convinced, they won't be. The pur-pose is even more important in virtual teams than it is in localized teams because we need the reminder of why we're doing what we're doing.

- (Name), I understand some of your resistance to the char-ter process. I'd like us to help you get past that—to find a way to make it work for you. It's part of our team-building and part of what creates trust to know exactly what we're committed to create and do, how we're committed to do it, and what we can count on you for.

- We have a broad mission for our charter. It's up to us to see if it makes sense. We can modify our own makeup to the extent that it clarifies the broader purpose and strategic intent we've been given.

Perfect Phrases to Discuss and Refine the Team Purpose

Refer back to the Section Two for a discussion of the team mission. That section helps define purpose in a general way. This section takes the description to a concrete level that virtual team members can commit to.

- Purpose starts at the top, but it isn't dictated by the top. As team leader, I'll open this discussion with the range and scope of our autonomy. I'll start with what's been handed down and proceed to where we have discretion.

- Let's go around the (virtual) room and answer these questions—why is this team important in your eyes? Why are you excited about being on this team? If you're not, tell us about your trepidation.

- Now let's go around the room and explain, each in our own words, why the mission of the team matters to the organization and the world.

- Let's break into (virtual) groups and take what we have heard to each create a draft charter. We want our charter to be clear, compelling, and comprehensive.

- (Name), you've been vocal about your resistance to this charter. Your concerns give us a launching pad for our discussion. Our goal—or one of them—is to create a statement of purpose that you can stand behind. When you and the team are ready, we'll invite you to present the draft charter statement to the whole group for us to ratify.

- Is that in alignment with stakeholder expectations as we understand them from the stakeholder questionnaire?

- Do we have consensus? Is this a purpose we can all work toward and with? All in favor say aye. All opposed say nay. We have a consensus. Time to celebrate! Then back to work. We've got a lot of teaming yet to do today!

Perfect Phrases to Differentiate Between Vision, Goals, and SMART Objectives

Professionals operate with different definitions of vision, goals, and objectives. You don't have to accept or adopt our definitions, but it will help you apply the phases if you understand how we use the terms. And it will help the team understand your processes if you explain how you use the terms. If you use different definitions, adapt the phrases to incorporate them.

- Because there are so many different definitions of visions, goals, and objectives, I'm beginning this section of our launch with working definitions of each.

- A vision describes a future state we aspire to achieve. It's a picture of what we want things to look like. Kind of like a future team portrait. It's the view.

- A virtual team vision paints a picture. That creates an image to strive toward.

- Goals are endpoints. Our stated goals define our target achievements. Think of the basketball hoop as the goal of a free throw. Our goals are like baskets. We might have to sink a lot of baskets to fulfill the charter purpose.

● The term *objective* comes from the word *object*, which means something in tangible form. Objectives make goals tangible. Our objectives will break our goals into concrete steps we'll take to reach our goals. To make a lot of baskets, we'll have to throw a lot of passes and block a lot of shots. That kind of thing.

● Objectives are clearly defined tasks to achieve the goals. They make goals concrete and actionable. They're specific, measurable, actionable, realistic, and time-bound. That spells SMART, and that acronym is a great test for how complete our objectives are.

● For example, a chain restaurant team established a mission to "Provide to valued customers prompt and high quality food and service in a friendly and courteous manner." Their stated vision is to be the number one restaurant chain in their market. Their goals include "Reduce the average customer waiting time by 10 minutes," "Reduce cholesterol in food by 10 percent within a year," and "Improve customer perception of courtesy within a year." They created objectives of adding six more tables to their dining rooms and adding a cook to each location during busy times by the end of the year.

Perfect Phrases to Establish Team Vision

Once the definition of terms is clear, guide your virtual team to fill in the details of this team vision with the following questions and phrases. At times the input will reveal differing understandings of what vision, goals, and objectives are. Use the

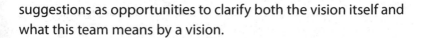

suggestions as opportunities to clarify both the vision itself and what this team means by a vision.

● What's our vision for this virtual team? How do we want to be known or seen?

    Our vision is our source of inspiration. If it doesn't inspire us, this will be drudgery. If it does, the hard work and striving will seem easier.

    If we take a cue from Martin Luther King and have a dream about this team, how would we describe it?

● Imagine we've come to the end of our work. We've fulfilled our purpose. How do we want to answer these questions:
    ● What are our sponsor and key stakeholders saying about the team?
    ● How can we accurately describe this team experience?

● Having a compelling vision is like having a ball we can keep our eyes on. We need it to hit the ball out of the park.

● What do you foresee as the most significant team legacy? Why?

    We all need a picture of what is possible for the team. A powerful vision is stronger than the space and time between us, and it focuses us on getting powerful results.

    Let's write the team assessment that you expect to see (your boss, the team sponsor, the clients, the customers) write (one year) from today.
    ● Now let's share.
    ● How can we combine our different visions?

- Is there anything about this vision that doesn't resonate with any of you?
- How can we rework it to address those concerns?

Can we set this as our virtual team vision?

Perfect Phrases to Establish Team Goals

Often by the launch, broad goals have been established. Even if goals are handed down in microscopic detail (which isn't preferable because it reduces the team's autonomy and intrinsic motivation), spend time reviewing, refining, and interpreting them.

Let's move on to our goals. We've been given the broad goals (mandated goals) of (explain goal mandates). We'll examine, refine them, and make them our own.

For our purposes, goals are end points, like crossing a finish line or sinking a free throw. What do we want to make happen?

Without compatible goals, we'll have competition, not cooperation.

Goals and measurements are like a virtual manager. They keep us focused on our important priorities. Then it isn't me or any member telling someone what he or she is doing isn't working. It's the results compared to the goal.

What finish line do we need to cross to fulfill our purpose? Or we could ask, what are our finish lines?

What would it mean to score a touchdown, hit the basket, or cross the finish line?

- How do we define success?

- Purpose leads to cooperative goals. These goals engender interdependent tasks that culminate in concrete results. It's do, doing, and done. We're defining the *do* part now.

- What specifically do we want to accomplish?

- Remember—a goal is a point, not a process. So if we have verbs, we'll rework them to describe the point of achievement. Our goals are our finish-line statements.

Tip and Warning!
Think of Your Team as
an Organism, Not a Machine

There is an organic quality to all teams. That includes the more prescriptive teams, and it is particularly true of creative teams. If you treat your team like a machine that you operate mechanically, you're likely to have major problems on your hands, and you certainly will limit creativity. Organisms evolve systemically and somewhat unpredictably. Who can predict where the next tree limb will emerge? A change in one aspect of an organism creates ripples in another. A team leader or boundary manager's job is to provide the conditions in which team members can learn and develop, and then get out of the way. It's more like being a gardener than an engineer (although my favorite engineers have organic ways of looking at their projects too). The guidelines here are intended to provide a foundation for creativity, not to create prisons of dos and don'ts that don't fit.

Perfect Phrases to Establish Virtual Team Objectives

Virtual team objectives are concrete. Objectives are about what you specifically do to achieve goals and live a vision and fulfill a purpose. You can alternate this discussion with the role discussion if desired. You might break into subgroups for some aspects of this process.

We touch on brainstorming here. For extensive brainstorming phrases, see *Perfect Phrases for Leadership Development* (Runion and Mack, McGraw-Hill, 2010).

- To supplement our virtual team charter, we received a detailed issue analysis. It's up to us to create a work plan to put it into action.

- The vision deploys into a set of goals, and each goal deploys into a set of objectives.
  - That means that if we meet all the goals, we achieve the vision. If we accomplish the objectives, we meet the goals.

- Let's identify objectives that pertain to each goal. Remember, objectives are the strategy to achieve the goals. They involve verbs and dates. For example, "Get site approval by June 13" is an *objective*.

- We have a goal of (pick one). What objectives will help us get there? Let's brainstorm ideas. We'll wait until later to evaluate them. This is an idea generation process.
  - What else?

- Do any of these ideas generate new ideas for anyone?

- We're using the acronym SMART objectives. Some people use the term *SMART goals*—I think it's more accurate to speak of SMART objectives. That means specific, measurable, actionable, realistic, and time-bound.
- Let's start with our first goal and explore strategies or objectives to make it happen.
- Now let's go through each objective and evaluate it to see if it's a SMART objective.
  - We'll start with the *S*, or *specific*. Is the objective clear? Concrete? Is there a lot of room for interpretation, or is it specific enough that we don't have confusion about what it is?
  - Next, is it measurable? If not, how can we make it measurable?
  - Can we tell from the definition whether we've succeeded in achieving it or not?
  - What test will tell us if we attained it?
  - Now, is it actionable? Are clear actions indicated in the objective?
  - Next, is it realistic? Is it attainable? It may be a stretch goal, but do we have a chance of making it happen?
  - Now, is it time-bound? Is there an exact time on it?
- Okay—we have objectives that fit the SMART definition. It's time to get the roles assigned.

Perfect Phrases to Define Tasks and Assign Roles and Responsibilities

People want to know what the work is and what is expected of them. These phrases clarify virtual team roles and responsibilities.

The phrases refer to a role matrix. A sample matrix is available at www.speakstrong.com/teams.

● One danger of virtual teams is thinking everyone needs to be involved in everything. That's a recipe for failure, so we're going to flesh out our responsibilities.

● I know you're all eager to know what your role will be. We'll start with an overview of the tasks, and then we'll look at who is responsible for what.

● I created a role matrix to make sure we all understand whom we report to, who reports to us, and who needs to be kept in the loop as we proceed. This is likely to morph as we evolve, so I'd like (name) to take responsibility for updating it and for us all to take responsibility for letting her know of any changes or inaccuracies.

● Your role for every task matters. The crucial roles are the ownership roles. Every task needs an owner.

● We selected you because of your expertise. We have a roles and responsibility matrix that (is filled in) (we need to fill in) to determine how to apply your expertise. It's not set in stone, but know that if you don't negotiate otherwise, when this meeting ends, your role on the chart is what you're expected to accomplish.

● If you are in doubt about whether a particular decision or activity requires collaboration, please err on the side of caution and ask. If anyone leaves you out of a collaboration that you should have been included on, let the person know and explain why it has your name on it.

Perfect Phrases to Introduce and Apply the Role Chart

A responsibility assignment matrix is an accountability structure to help virtual team members know how to work together and communicate progress. The form varies from RASCI to RACI to CAIRO to DACI. If you have a standard role chart, adapt these phrases to it. The acronym RACING can work well because it both defines the roles and is easy to remember. Use these phrases to introduce the structures you plan to use.

- Our role matrix includes the letters R-A-C-I-N-G. Think of it as a tool that guides us in racing to successful outcomes. You can see the role chart on the screen.

- We'll use it to assign roles to tasks, not just for us but also for stakeholders and others who need to be kept in the loop about what we're doing.

- *R* means *responsible*. That's the person who does the work.

- *A* means *approver*. You're the one who signs off on the work. It's not up to you to do the work, just to oversee that it's done. The approver is the person who has ultimate responsibility for the task. An *A* by any task means you own it.

- *C* means *consulted*. This person is a resource. He or she can advise, but not veto.

- *I* means *informed*. That's the people or groups who need to be notified of results or actions but don't need to be involved in the decision-making process. The team keeps the *I*s updated. No response is necessary.

N means *not involved*. Out of the loop. If someone has an *N* where his or her name and the task intersect, there is no need to update the person or involve him or her with that task in any way. Don't cc this person on e-mail updates.

G means *group*. A *G* task is everyone's responsibility, and accountability is structured into our group processes. We're all responsible, for example, for making the team chat feed relevant.

All together it spells *RACING*, which is what we're doing— racing to successful outcomes.

We'll create our chart in our team project files. We'll identify and list all of the tasks involved in the project down the vertical axis of the spreadsheet.

Now, all of the people and roles involved in the project are listed across the horizontal axis.

Okay—let's go through and identify the R, A, C, I, N, and G for each task on your vertical axis.

Where are there gaps in our matrix? What tasks and activities don't have an *R*? We need someone doing the work for each task.

- Where are the overlaps? Do we see multiple *R*s in places?
  - Do we need to break some of those tasks into subtasks?
  - Who needs to see our RACING chart for feedback before we make final revisions and get started on the project?
  - We'll send the link to the chart to those people.
- We'll create our team dashboard in our (example: project management software). You can use the dashboard

to create a personal dashboard as well. Who needs dashboard training?

- The dashboard highlights our progress so we can see at a glance if we are on track or ahead of goal, making progress but not on target, or falling significantly behind on our goal.

- At first we'll need to review our progress more frequently. We'll start out on a weekly basis and scale back once we get our flow going.

- Please update your metrics daily or whenever there is any notable progress. We're each responsible for our own updates and for checking in to see how the tasks we're depending on are going.

- When someone falls behind on a task, people who sign up for notices will get automatic updates.

CHAPTER 8

Define and Align the Virtual Team Culture

What you do is important. How you do it is also important. This section is about deciding how to play well with each other.

Perfect Phrases to Initiate a Dynamically Aligned Culture

Establish a deliberate culture to minimize cultural collisions that sabotage your virtual team effectiveness. Culture is behaviors and beliefs characteristic of a particular group. Cultural difference can result from age, department, nationality, gender, or many other differences, including differences in thinking. Virtual teams struggle most with the collision between adaptive and maintaining mindsets. If you hired for adaptability, your team members will have the temperament required to turn cultural differences into opportunities.

- We're a blend of cultures, and our challenge is to align the cultures we have into a deliberate team culture. Otherwise we'll be in a world of hurt over (be fighting) different ideas of how to be with each other.

- Culture is learned behavior about how to work together. It's our norms—written and verbal, conscious and unconscious. How do we want to communicate, work together, solve problems, and make decisions? What behaviors can we count on from each other? What agreements will help us work together effectively to achieve our goals?

- The one underlying cultural attitude we need to share is a bias toward adaptiveness and collaboration. If we can be adaptive with each other, we can align and turn our differences into our advantage.

- We have partners and suppliers on this virtual team. We have executives and engineers on this team. We have people from all over the world. We each have different individual goals. Our challenge is to integrate them.
    - What other cultural differences do we have?

- You'd think the day shift and night shift would have very similar cultures. Do they?
    - What cultural differences could affect our team?

- We're setting timelines. I know that even with collocated teams, we can have different ideas of what that means. Let's go around geographically and answer some questions about how we regard timelines—understanding that we are sharing our viewpoints rather than seeking a correct answer.

- If you promise to send someone something on May 13, what is the latest exact time you could send it and be honoring your word?
- If you have a lunch date at 12 noon, what range of arrival time do you consider acceptable?

- What does face-saving mean in your culture?
  - How can we respect the value of that quality while we learn from each other and identify the source of our problems?

- Let's talk about directness. What is an appropriate way to disagree in your culture?
  - How do you explore and share ideas if your culture doesn't support disagreeing?
  - How will we disagree in the virtual team culture we're creating?

- We've explored our differences. Our next step is to create a team operating agreement that keeps us dynamically aligned and moving forward.

- If you sense a clash between team culture and what you're comfortable with, please speak up. We'll all need to adapt to each other, but we don't want anyone to feel like he or she is violating an important value.

Perfect Phrases to Establish Social Dynamic Goals

You set the tangibles (goals and objectives) you want to achieve. Now, step back and establish social dynamic goals. These goals will guide your next step in developing more specific operating agreements and norms. Revisit this section and your social dynamic goals periodically—especially when the team hits a rough spot.

- Moving from collocated teams to a virtual team is as much or more a human event as a technological one. If we miss that, we set ourselves up for problems.

- Think about the best team, virtual or otherwise, you've been on. Name five behaviors that contributed to the success of the team. Let's discuss it.
  - Let's set social dynamics goals that reflect what we like about what we heard.

- What kinds of fears and frustrations do you have around the social aspect of our virtual team?
  - I'll start—(example: sometimes I'm concerned some members will interpret my questions as a sign of weakness rather than a proactive attempt to get clarity).
  - Who's next?

- The goal of managing our tasks is productivity. The goal of managing our social dynamics is unity. What are some of the social dynamic challenges we encounter on virtual teams?

- Let's talk about inclusion.
  - What kind of challenges are there around inclusion?
  - What kind of goals can we set to be inclusive as a team?

- Position and status can be confusing if we aren't clear up front.
  - What can we do to be as clear as possible about position and status?
  - What kind of goals can we set to make sure those concerns are handled?

- Power always plays into social dynamics and, along with it, resource allocation. Let's talk about our goals in the area of power and resource allocation.
  - What kind of power dynamics do we want on the team?
  - What kind of power dynamics do we want to avoid?
  - How will we manage ineffective or destructive power dynamics?
- We'll need to manage participation. Let's set a goal for the kind of interaction and participation we want.
  - How will we encourage that kind of interaction?
  - Are we all in agreement that if someone isn't stepping up to the plate, we all have responsibility to engage him or her?
- Let's talk about trust. Trust is vital for virtual team success. Without trust the team won't experience sustained collaboration and we'll eventually self-destruct.
  - What causes you to trust someone?
  - What behaviors can destroy trust?
- How do you confront someone on the team who has violated your trust? How do you get trust back on track?
- Okay. We have a list of social dynamic goals to refer to as we establish our operating agreements.

Perfect Phrases to Establish Meeting Norms

Seek agreement on meeting practices with the following questions and phrases. To simplify and streamline this process, the team leader can recommend a format and open it for improvement suggestions. Circulate or post the starting guidelines for comment during prelaunch. You'll find a sample team meeting norm list at www.speakstrong.com.

- Let's talk about meetings. Our meeting needs may shift as we develop, but let's get in agreement on key issues.

- First, let's look at how often we should meet. In the prelaunch memo I proposed (weekly for the first month). I received some input and have refined that recommendation to (example: Monday at 8 a.m. As we get more clarity about roles, milestones, etc., we'll meet only when we need to.). Are there any objections or refinements to that?

- I'd like to set a goal of reducing our formal meeting times as quickly as we can without compromising our productivity. The quicker we get up to speed on using our collaborative technologies, the fewer full team meetings we'll need.

- Next, let's look at how we'll decide to call unscheduled meetings. I don't want to be the only one to do that, so I opened the topic for input during the prelaunch. Based on the input I received, I recommend (example: when there is a milestone event coming up, milestone completions, urgent team decisions, etc.).

- How shall we decide which medium to use for each meeting? What's worked in the past for me has been (recommendation).
  - Does that work for you?
- What's our meeting attendance policy?
  - What's a legitimate reason to miss a meeting, and how will we handle absences?

- We'll go over a list of guidelines for effective meeting protocol in a minute. Those won't just be for efficiency—they'll be to make meetings so dynamic that no one will choose to miss without very good reason.

- Our software for meeting notification is (example: Outlook). Are we all able to accept meetings that way? Is there anyone who will need a minitutorial for it?
  - Who can walk (name) through meeting requests and acceptances?

- Let's talk about time zones and meetings. What blocks of time are preferred for each member? Which blocks of time won't work?

- I've posted a draft of proposed meeting norms. Let's discuss adaptations.

- Now you'll see a draft of meeting formats. Let's discuss adaptions.

- Have we refined our meeting norms?

Perfect Phrases to Establish Decision-Making Norms

It sounds a bit paradoxical to say that you need to make a decision about how to make decisions. You do. These phrases will help.

- Who has operated on a team that was highly effective in making decisions?
  - How did you do it?

- (Activity) Here's an activity for us. I need one person who favors (one option, example, one messaging format over another) and one person who favors (an opposing option).
  - Sit across this table from each other. (Or imagine sitting across the table from each other.) Get in arm wrestling position. Now go!
  - Okay, we'll go with the winner's preference. Makes sense, doesn't it?
  - Of course we wouldn't make an important decision by arm wrestling. However, that's what we do when we let the most aggressive person or the person with the loudest voice drive our decisions. If anyone wants that to be our official method of making decisions, let me know. Otherwise, let's continue and we'll discuss how we will actually make decisions.

- Who has ever felt that decisions or a decision was made by an ineffective method?
  - What was it?

- Before we get into procedures to make decisions, let's create a statement about the underlying basis for decisions, remembering why we're here in the first place. Sometimes teams default into guidelines like "Our decisions reflect the stubbornness of our more vocal members and the fears of our more accommodating members." Let's pick guidelines to strive for so we won't default into something like that.

  - What ultimately guides every decision?
  - How can we state that clearly? (Example: every decision is guided by our purpose of delivering a quality product on schedule.)

- Great! Now, how will we solve problems and make decisions?
    - How do we keep our purpose and vision in sight when we make decisions?
    - How will we ensure decisions incorporate the expertise of each member?
- How do our roles and responsibilities affect our decision autonomy?
    - How will we decide when to include the group in a decision? For example, as team leader and boundary manager, I act as a buffer between external stakeholders and the team. My role of creating the conditions for you to do your jobs will guide my decisions on your behalf. I invite feedback if my decisions interfere rather than aid your success.
    - Can you think of particular categories of decisions that you generally prefer I make for the team? Any that you want to be sure you are at least consulted on?
    - How can we each exercise our autonomy while ensuring team members get input on decisions that affect them?
- I suggest when we have decisions that affect the team or other team members and we have any question about the appropriateness of a unilateral decision, we send out queries or surveys with the option that the decision be kicked up to the team level.
- Let's decide who has the authority to make unilateral decisions on what issues and how we communicate those decisions.

- For team decisions, I propose a consensus-based decision-making process.
  - A request for consensus begins with a proposal, clarification, open floor for discussion, and call for consensus.
  - If we don't reach consensus, we'll address all concerns, submit changes if offered, and make a second call for consensus.
  - If we still don't have consensus, we'll discuss each unresolved concern in detail and submit it for a third call for consensus.
  - If we still don't have consensus, we'll write a summary documenting the issues and circulate it to (example: informed sponsors) for review.
  - Remember, consensus doesn't mean unanimous support. You just need to not feel morally or ethically violated by it and be willing to actively support the decision.

Perfect Phrases to Set Response Time and Availability Norms

The name of the virtual team game is dynamic collaboration, which is enhanced by immediacy of feedback. Team members need to know how to reach each other quickly with urgent questions.

- We ask all team members to keep their team desktop chat open as much as possible to be available for immediate information sharing when time matters.

- We know we each have many demands on our time. We also know the team is committed to effectively delivering our objectives on time. So let's talk about our availability. This includes participating in team meetings, preparing for meetings and completing assigned tasks, and responding to inquiries. Let's create availability norms.

- Now let's translate that into individual response time and availability agreements. It's about when and how we can be reached individually and how quickly we will respond.

- Availability agreements help us all know what we can count on from each other. Sometimes knowing when someone might get back to us is more important than getting a quick response.
    - There are three components of every response: message received, understood, and acted on. You might agree to respond to receiving all messages within 24 hours to at least state when you'll be able to give a more complete response.

- Your commitments may be different from mine because of your circumstances and team role.
    - Let's go around alphabetically and discuss each role and what kind of availability concerns we have for that role. For example, our team technician is someone I would like to know I can reach quickly during normal business hours and on a preagreed emergency basis for high-stakes events, even if it's off hours in her time zone. (Name of person in the role), does that work for you?

- Based on the feedback we've received and what's possible, let's each create our own commitments based on what is needed and appropriate to our role on the team. We'll post these for everyone to see, so make sure it's realistic.
  - I'll go first with an example. I commit to responding to all communication within 24 hours and urgent communication at my next available opportunity. I check voice mail twice a day and e-mail morning and afternoon. I can be texted or called at home for emergencies—anything that you need an immediate answer for.
- Now it's time to set a priority communication medium—one we all agree to monitor closely. We don't want to have to notify individuals separately or take the time to look up everyone's preferences in an emergency. Will it be texting, voice mail, or the team feed?

Perfect Phrases to Set E-mail Norms

The best way to handle e-mail overload is to go to the cloud and handle more communication through blogs, chats, document sharing with notification, and other team network applications. Additionally, your e-mail client features, such as mail rules, can do much of the sorting for you.

- Let's talk about e-mail. We want it to serve us, not the other way around. A lively way to start this conversation is to talk about our e-mail pet peeves. You name 'em and I'll post 'em on the (virtual) whiteboard.

Before we dive into a conversation about what *to* do, let's see if there are pet peeves that we can agree we *won't* do straight out before going into detail.

First, put the team name (or if it's long, an agreed-upon acronym) at the beginning of the subject line so team members can easily create e-mail rules for team communication.

Next, put the people who need to act on an e-mail in the "To" column and cc those who receive the e-mail as FYIs (for information only). Again, we can set our mail rules to sort those e-mails for us.

Also, we have distribution lists for e-mail categories. If a group needs to take action on an e-mail, list the group name in the "To" column. If you're sending an e-mail to a group, for example, stakeholders, just for their information, put the group distribution list in the cc column.

When you sign up for a team distribution list, you can specify whether you want to receive team notifications in separate e-mails or a daily digest.

To minimize e-mail and maximize transparency, most of our discussions will be online. That way everyone sees the questions and everyone can read the responses. You can register for e-mail notifications of discussions and opt in for individual notifications of individual posts to specific discussions.

We'll notify you when we post documents of interest to individuals or subgroups. Please subscribe to updates and notifications of when the relevant documents have been updated.

Tip and Warning!
Let Immediacy Work for You—Not Against You

Be really careful with "reply all." It can get you in a lot of trouble! E-mail and immediacy will work for you *if* you pause just long enough to determine that the response you are sending is one you will be glad you sent later and the recipients will be glad to receive. Sometimes taking a few moments saves a lot of time.

Not hitting "reply all" can cause problems too. Once the team is into an e-mail thread, if someone fails to "reply all," some of the team is out of the loop and may miss a critical comment. Plus they might wonder if they weren't included because there was a comment about them. Of course, posting to team discussions keeps everything transparent.

Perfect Phrases to Establish Conflict and Disagreement Norms

It's not about *if* conflict comes up, it's about *when*. Conflict is anything that needs to be worked through for team effectiveness. If you work through conflict early, you can resolve it before anyone really considers it to be a battle. Create agreements that turn conflict into opportunities. You can find a conflict disagreement norm at www.speakstrong.com.

- Conflict happens. When it does, I ask each of you to:
  - Identify potential conflicts early.

- Be clear and direct about what you see as the issues or positions in the conflict.
- Suggest a number of alternatives for resolving the conflict if these are apparent to you.
- Ask the group to begin this process if alternatives are not apparent to you.
- Respect both truth and grace while working to resolve the conflict.
- Say what you mean and mean what you say, without being mean when you say it.
- Speak up if you have something to say that can move the group toward a constructive resolution.
- Observe quietly if you don't have something to say that can move the group toward a constructive resolution.
- Support the team decision as we move beyond the conflict.

- My list is on the whiteboard. Let's discuss it as a whole and then go over each item for consensus.

- Here is the list with our adaptations and adjustments. Are we good with this list?
  - Do we have consensus?
  - Is everyone willing to operate this way, or to renegotiate the way we handle conflict if the agreement seems to face obstacles?
  - Remember, this is a real commitment, and we will bring this out when we have conflict.

- If an issue can't be resolved via e-mail in two rounds, the team members agree to try to resolve it by phone. And if

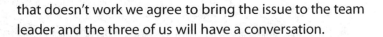

that doesn't work we agree to bring the issue to the team leader and the three of us will have a conversation.

Perfect Phrases to Establish the Team Identity

You've come a long way by now. Your group is becoming a team. Take steps to establish team identity. Choose a name, brand the team, and note any exclusivity that comes with being a member of the team.

- I say we're ready for our team name. Our team founders have been using (name) to refer to us. We're ready to name ourselves now.
  - A team name is a mental model and symbolizes our identity. We could start with a formal name related to our purpose—or we could see what bubbles up. Who has a nickname for the team already? Let's brainstorm.
  - What do we like?
  - Is there anyone who is put off by that name? It's important that our team name is working for all of us.
  - Okay, our official team name is (name).
- Who'd like to draft a team logo?
  - What starter ideas do we have for a team logo? Just a simple word logo is fine.
  - Do any images come to mind?
- Let's take a look at team tagline ideas—something that sums up our team purpose in a few words.

- If the team had a bumper sticker, what would it say?

- Members of (team name) have access to privileged information in our backstage areas. Once we get a team logo and tagline, we'll use them.

- We're establishing our (team name) public face and a (team name) backstage virtual area where we'll meet, discuss options, make decisions, and resolve conflict. We're transitioning from a group to a team.

CHAPTER 9

Summarize and Finalize Team Formation

Perfect Phrases to Identify and Manage Key Team Stakeholders

Who is affected by the work of the team? From customers to managers to suppliers and colleagues, identify and prepare to manage key stakeholders during the launch. This includes shared stakeholders—people with an interest in the team as a whole—and unique stakeholders, such as family and supervisors for other team members who will be influenced by the fact that this person is on the team.

- To keep our stakeholders informed, we have a stakeholder group page on our team site. It has the information that all stakeholders want and need to know.

- If we don't manage our communication with and expectations of our stakeholders, it'll come back to bite us. That's next on the launch agenda.

- We have stakeholder feedback questionnaires and feedback forms from the stakeholders involved in the team formation. We'll start by addressing their expectations and requirements. They aren't the only stakeholders, however. Anyone who's affected by the existence of the team is a stakeholder, potentially including your grandmother, assistant, and certainly anyone you directly report to. We'll get to them after the team stakeholders.

- We have documentation of key team stakeholder expectations. Let's discuss each one and revisit our stated goals and objectives and make sure these expectations are addressed.
  - Do we need to revisit our plan to better address stakeholder expectations?
  - As boundary manager, I'm ultimately responsible for managing key stakeholder expectations. Which stakeholders will I do that directly with? For which stakeholders does it make more sense for a team member to manage the relationship directly, with my support?
  - Are all the team stakeholders properly represented on the RACING chart?
  - Do we know who is responsible for managing communication with each stakeholder?
  - Let's discuss each one in terms of power and influence and explore who we see as potential allies or detractors.
  - What will we do if a stakeholder disagrees with the team's decisions?

- A good rule is, we will vigorously discuss conflict during team meetings, but consensus will be solidly supported outside team meetings. That includes with our stake-holders. Can we all commit to that?

● What documents from this meeting will we want to share with our key stakeholders?

● You each have individual stakeholders. I invited you to identify them before the launch. Now let's answer the same questions about these personal stakeholders that we addressed as a group regarding team stakeholders.

● We'll need to answer the following questions for each of our personal stakeholders.
  ● Do they understand the importance of the team?
  ● Have you discussed the purpose with them?
  ● Have they expressed concerns? What are they?
  ● What do your personal stakeholders need from you?

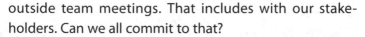

Perfect Phrases to Assemble the Team Charter

Hooray! You've got the pieces to put the team charter together. If you've done your work well, this part of the process is as simple as filling in the charter form, and voilà—you have a road map. You'll find a sample at www.speakstrong.com/team. Fill the phrase in with the summaries you developed earlier.

● We're ready for the fun part: assembling and ratifying our team charter. This is where we really become a team. Our meeting scribe will walk us through each section and we'll put it together.

Our team name is…

The purpose of our team is to (purpose statement from earlier in the meeting).

Our vision is to…

We share the goals of…

Our chair and coordinator is…

Our core members are…

Extended members are…

Stakeholders include…

The scope and boundaries of our team are…

Our key deliverables are…

We will measure success by…

On to our operating norms.
- Our meeting norms are…
- Our decision-making norms are…
- Our response time and availability norms are…
- Our e-mail norms are…
- Our disagreement and conflict management norms are…
- Our key stakeholder management norms are…

That'll do it. Let's look it over and make sure there isn't anything we overlooked. Then we can ratify it as a team, and we have our charter! Our team has a road map!

Perfect Phrases to Close the Team Launch and Team Formation Process

You've got your road map. You're ready to close and send the team off for the next stage in the team's life. A good closing energizes the team members as they make the transition to task-related work.

- It's transition time. We'll wrap up by summarizing and reviewing the action plan. We'll discuss what learning has come from this exercise, and then we'll celebrate!

- We want to leave with a clear action plan. That doesn't mean we predetermine every step. The next steps for subgroups often are to create their own action plans. If we have completed these steps effectively, this process will be as simple as filling out a form.

- Let's finalize our action plan. It's who will do what by when.
  - For starters, I'll prepare and post the launch summary. You'll find it at (location).
  - What has been added since we went through our objective and task session?
  - I'd like someone to laminate and distribute our team norms. We'll have them online, but we also should have them in our wallets or at our desks.
  - What else needs to be added to our initial lists?

- Let's go around by location and summarize the commitments we made.

- In review, is everything clear and accurate?

- Who'll format and post the action plan?
- Let's each share one thing we learned or appreciate about this team. Or both! I'll go first. I learned (example: great ways to organize e-mail), and I appreciate the willingness of this team to stick it out, even when things seem murky.
- I say we've moved from being a group to a team. Let's close with one word each about what that means for each of us.

PART III

TEAMING

SECTION 4

Guide and Grow

Congratulations! You've gone from being a group to a team! The attention shifts from building a foundation to working upon that foundation.

Virtual teams continue to evolve toward becoming leaderless. That gives teams the opportunity to be leader-*full*. In great functioning virtual teams, leaders step forward and back according to the need of the situation. Even if you don't have "lead" or "manage" in your official role, the phrases in these sections will help you and your virtual team succeed.

CHAPTER 10

Provide Focus and Support

The early stages of team operation require emphasis on focus and support. The learning curve is high just to get rolling. At times it feels like the ball is rolling backward, but if you did your launch well, you have clear purpose, vision, goals, objectives, and operating agreements to focus and support your team.

Perfect Phrases to Describe the Boundary Manager's Role

Team management involves working on the team structure both from the outside and from within that structure. We refer to working from outside as boundary management and within as team leadership. Boundary managers work *on* the system that the rest of the team works *in*. If your team doesn't have a boundary manager who understands and executes that role, you might need to fill some of the gap and step outside the system to see what the team needs, even if that's not your official responsibility. We all can get lost inside a system.

Imagine the virtual team always meets inside of a particular conference room. I, as boundary manager, stand in the doorway of that room, managing the flow of information into and out of the room. I work to minimize distractions from entering the room. I facilitate helpful information entering the room. And I work, perhaps like a publicist, to help the work of the team be seen in the best light as it leaves the room.

It's my job to manage the boundaries—the interface with other teams, customers, and the whole list of stakeholders. I run interference when external influences get in the way of your being able to do your job. It's also my job to help you get the tools and training you need to be successful.

If anything in the system puts obstacles in your path, I'm the go-to person for that. That's the role of a boundary manager.

I notice many of you are getting external e-mails that don't relate to you directly. To shield you from inappropriate distraction and unnecessary confusion, I'll intercept and filter what I can so what arrives in your inbox is relevant.

As boundary manager, I'll introduce you to the key external contacts.

I'm bringing in some external customer feedback for your review. It will help guide our next step.

As the boundary manager, it's my job to keep an eye on the big picture and coordinate the pieces. It's also my job to help team members keep the big picture in mind as they proceed. I'm not going to tell you how to do your job, but if I think I can help you focus so you can find a better direction for yourself, that's what I'll do.

● As the boundary manager, I don't work in the system; I work *on* the system to make it as functional as possible. We worked hard to create a foundation for the team. That doesn't mean it's perfect. They say no battle plan ever outlasts first contact with the enemy. So if the foundation we built seems to be getting in the way of functioning, let me know.

● At minimum, you need the tools to do your work to the satisfaction of the customer. It's my job to make sure you have them. If any of you are doing work-arounds because you don't have the tools to do your jobs correctly, I need to know about it.

● The boundary manager's role is to make sure processes that lead to good teaming are in place. It's not to control the processes.

Perfect Phrases to Discuss the Team Leader and Team Member Role

The team leader works within the system to monitor progress, coordinate activities, and otherwise guide activities for successful execution. Increasingly, the leadership baton passes from member to member based on tasks and specific expertise.

● As your team leader, I'm responsible for the results even when the situation calls for someone else to take control of the ball, whether because of expertise or some other reason.

● As your virtual team *leader*, I have a responsibility to develop each and every one of you. As a virtual team *member*, I have a technical contribution to this decision that I want you to consider on its own merits, not by consideration of my leader role.

- I'm boundary manager, team leader, and team member. I have different functions in each role, so I'll make a distinction between them as I see the need and value.

- It's part of my role as team leader to build links between team members. I notice a few of you aren't communicating as much as would benefit the project. To help create those links, I'll (example: start a discussion on the site that I'd like each of you to contribute to).

- I make decisions for the team to keep from bogging everyone down with having to make every little decision themselves. If I misjudge and make a decision that should have been a team decision, I want to hear about it.

- My commitment is to lead and manage to benefit the team as a whole. If anything I do seems to be unilaterally imposed, tell me.

- It seems the team needs resources we don't have. I'll talk to the boundary manager about that.

Perfect Phrases to Anchor Launch Agreements and Action Steps

Anchor the launch agreements and keep them living, growing, and vital. One of the best ways you can anchor agreements is to practice them, so be impeccable about modeling the agreements as you remind your team of them.

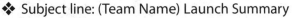

- ❖ Subject line: (Team Name) Launch Summary
  - ❖ Body: Dear (team name) members. Thanks so much for your participation in our team launch. We've accomplished so much that some of us might be overwhelmed. To simplify and anchor what we agreed on, I'm (sending out/linking to) our summary documents. Watch for follow-up e-mails and reminders. I'll send out notices all week to reinforce all the good work we did last week. You have every document you need from this notice, but I'll highlight each one in the course of the next week to get us off on the best foot. Don't worry— I'll communicate often, but each message will be brief.

- ❖ Subject line: (Team Name) Prioritization Codes and Posting Guidelines
  - ❖ Body: New habits take time to develop. Once we all get into the habit of using our agreed-upon prioritization codes, it will save us time and confusion. I've pasted the codes below, and you can find them posted here: (link). Come to our meeting (time, virtual location) prepared to talk about how the prioritization codes are working for you so far.

- ❖ Subject line: (Team Name) Deliverables, Roles, and Responsibilities
  - ❖ Body: Do you know who is responsible for what? The team roles and responsibilities matrix is posted (location). Please review it to make sure it accurately reflects your understanding of what we agreed to and what the project requires. It (has/hasn't) been updated since the launch. Please register online for automatic updates

regarding changes in particular roles and responsibilities. You need to know this stuff.

❖ Subject Line: (Team Name) Response and Availability Norms
  ❖ Body: Ever wonder about the best time and method to reach a team member? You can find that information on every team member's page, in addition to the availability chart posted (location). While you're reviewing your team members' pages, check out your own, too, and make sure the information is accurate. As a small incentive, there's a deliberate typo in one of the profiles. The first person who catches it gets an online gift certificate. If there are typos that aren't deliberate, I budgeted to give a few certificates away for them, too. You'll find out who was the first to find them at the next team meeting at (time, virtual location).

❖ Subject Line: (Team Name) Stakeholder Management
  ❖ Body: We created lists of key team stakeholders and individual member stakeholders. Have you shared the launch results with your individual stakeholders? Have you established understandings, agreements, and norms with people who will be affected by the team? Who has a story to share with the team about what you've done to get your individual stakeholders on board? Save those stories and challenges for our next virtual team meeting at (time, virtual location).

❖ Subject line: (Team Name) Purpose
  ❖ Body: It's easy to get involved in our work and forget why we're here. So here's a quick reminder of our purpose as a team. We defined it as (purpose statement) and summarized that in the tagline (tagline).

- (Name), how was the launch meeting for you?
  - Is there any confusion around it?
  - What did you like most about it?
  - Is there anything that didn't seem complete when you reflected on it afterward?
  - Are all our agreements clear, or is there something that you would like help interpreting into action?
- We did the best we could to anticipate and head off problems in the launch meeting, but we all know challenges will emerge as we get to know each other. If any of our agreements and action steps need improvement once we shine the light of implementation on them, let me know!

Perfect Phrases to Build Virtual Team Trust

Trust isn't about being best friends. It's about action. One professional noted, "I don't need my team member to share his childhood traumas or hopes and dreams with me. I just need to know he'll return my calls."

These phrases guide and facilitate trust. Don't use them to mask actions that betray trust. The next section on encouraging personal interaction is also useful for building trust.

- My commitment is to be open with you. To be honest. To share good news and bad. To be straightforward about my actions and intentions. To admit my mistakes. To be responsive to your requests. Trust takes time to build and can be lost in an instant. I cherish your trust and intend to protect it.
  - Let's each explain how we expect to earn the trust of the team.

- I heard a speaker say that trust grows when the range of subjects we share with someone grows. The more topics we talk about, the more we come to trust each other. I have a different view. To me, trust grows when we feel we *can* talk about things that matter and not regret it. If I ever send a signal that it's not safe to talk to me about something that matters, please let me know.
  - What kind of behaviors build trust for you?
  - What destroys trust?

- Let's open this meeting by reminding ourselves of our commitment to confidentiality. As a team, we need to be able to trust that what we say and discuss here will stay private. As far as team members who weren't able to be here today, we're committed to speak in the same way we would if they were here, and to refer them to the source if anything comes up today they need to know about. We speak *to* team members, not *about* them. Agreed?

- Our goal is total trust. We're human, so we're not there yet. But let's start by asking—what stands between you and the ability to trust this team? What are the obstacles, and how can we remove them?
  - Here's one guideline for the team as a whole. Don't make team members guess what you're thinking. Tell them. That's the kind of disclosure that trust is built on.

- Let's talk about open communication—what it means for this team. I think a lot of us get confused and think it means a kind of verbal diarrhea. Sometimes we take it to mean dumping. What do we as a team mean when we consider open communication and trust?

- Virtual teams are based on trust. We start from trust. We get trust by giving trust. If any of us experience doubt, we need to be open about communicating that. That's part of trust.

- I received your suggestion about (suggestion), and I responded by (action). Thanks for the recommendation.

- Thanks for confiding in me. This is information I need to be able to manage the team. Let's talk about the kind of confidentiality you require with this.

Tip and Warning!
Consciously and Deliberately Feed Trust

It's harder to trust what you don't understand and can't see. Start from a position of trust, and be impeccable in being trustworthy yourself at every point. Help team members become aware of how their behaviors might undermine trust. Team members really want to know:

1. Will team members deliver as they say they will, or do I need to protect myself with a contingency plan? (This trust requires confidence in both expertise and delivery estimates.)

2. Can I speak openly in a genuine effort to clear obstacles that stand between me or us and success, or will team members misinterpret my efforts at clarity by taking offense?

3. Can I admit where I'm still learning and unclear, or will team members interpret questions and confusion as a

(continued)

sign of weakness and unprofessionalism? Might they respond to my transparency by showing off their "superior knowledge"?

4. Can I/we share my ideas and efforts freely, or will a team member grandstand and claim my/our hard work as his or her own?

Perfect Phrases for Personalized Interaction

Many people don't welcome personalization for its own sake, so tie personalization in with the project and be brief. Quick, light touches at the beginning of team meetings or periodic e-mails can add a personal and "high touch" dynamic to the "high tech" virtual team environment.

- Most of us like getting a sense of the environment team members work in. Let's submit pictures of our work environments for our team member pages and our next virtual meeting.

- Let's also post our birthdays, anniversary dates, children's pictures, etc., to keep us connected.

- Please attach your photo to everything you post to the team site. That way we can see you when we read what you write.

- We'll post the team photo we took at our off-site team launch. We Photoshopped a few of us in there who missed the launch.

- Since (name) doesn't have a web cam, we're posting his picture when he speaks. That way we'll have a visual with our audio.
  - When any team member speaks, we'll put his or her profile picture on the screen. Here's a composite of all the pictures. Some of us have animals and kids as our profile pictures. Who will tell us about the picture he or she selected?

Let's get up close and personal with the camera. We want to see you full frame!

(Name), last time we spoke you mentioned (event, activity, challenge, etc.). Before we get to business, how'd it go?

- Who has a win to share with the group before we continue?

- Anyone facing a challenge he or she'd like the team to be aware of before we get to the agenda?

- We asked everyone to share photos of where they work. I have them on my screen (I posted them on the intranet, SlideShare, etc.), and before we get to our main agenda, let's review them. We'll go around and talk about our setups.
  - After seeing this, who else wants to hang up now and reorganize your setup?

Each week we'll do a brief exchange to get to know others' styles. This week let's start with a three-minute description of a favorite software, new app, or technology.

Next week we'll do our getting-to-know-each-other exercise about communication styles. To prepare, please take the communication inventory at www.speakstrong.com/inventory (DiSC or other style inventories).

- We updated our internal social media site with new pics, announcements, etc. Who wants to share something interesting or meaningful that happened since our last meeting?

- (Name), you sound excited about what you're telling us. How does that tap into your interest?

- Hi, (name)! I'm headed home and am calling to see how you're doing and if there's anything you need from me on the project.

Tip and Warning!
Don't Get or Allow Team Members
to Get Machiavellian

Most virtual team communication is task-directed and purposeful. Without spontaneous water-cooler rapport building, it's easy to reduce people to their function and to what you want from them. Watch for signs of team members—including you—becoming utilitarian with each other. Use team building at the first sign of cunning and manipulation. Behavior that uses trickery and suggests a member of the team is more interested in her own well-being undermines the successful functioning of the team as a whole.

Perfect Phrases for the Premeeting Virtual Team Agenda

A preliminary draft agenda is a valuable virtual team management tool. Send out a premeeting agenda for input and comments. That will give everyone a say, help you identify missed areas, and allow the team to prepare. The fundamental guide for meeting productivity is the acronym PAL—purpose, agenda, and length.

- ❖ Subject line: (Team Name) Team Meeting Agenda for (Date/Time)
  - ❖ Body: I've (attached/posted) the preliminary agenda for our meeting scheduled for (date and time, virtual location).
  - ❖ Please let me know what input and suggestions you have.
  - ❖ Some helpful steps for preparing are (steps).
- ❖ Subject line: (Team Name) Meeting Preparation for (Date/Time)
  - ❖ We will (example: review our milestones and deliverables) at the next meeting of (team name). To prepare, please (example: update our "scorecard" accordingly).
- ❖ Subject line: Team Meeting Agenda: Call for Input
  - ❖ Body: I plan to finalize and circulate the agenda for our (team name) meeting (date). If you have issues that you need input on or that affect more than one of our team members, please let me know how much time you'll need and whether you want input or a decision.

Perfect Phrases to Assign and Manage Virtual Team Meeting Prep Work

Meeting prep work helps team members take full advantage of the meeting by thinking ahead and preparing. Well thought out prep-work assignments prime attendees for active and open participation in the real-time event. They also prepare the facilitator (the team leader or rotated member) to manage the session effectively and help you focus questions and stimulate ideas. Prep work needs to be value-added and seen as an integral part of the team's work. Make prep-work expectations clear.

❖ Prep work for our next meeting:
  ❖ The first item on the (team name) meeting agenda is prep work. Each member's completion of the assignment will prepare us for a more efficient and productive meeting. You'll find your prep-work assignment posted at (location).
  ❖ The prep work involves (examples: logging in to the team site, reading a white paper, implementing a recommendation in it, and summarizing the results on the online meeting space/taking a tutorial on the groupware and identifying the key features that we need to be proficient in as a team).
  ❖ I estimate the prep work will take (example: 15 to 30 minutes). If you have questions, post a comment on the site (e-mail, call, ask me for help).
  ❖ There is a small group exercise at (link location). I've assigned (teams/partners) for this exercise. I'll ask you to report your results at the meeting.
❖ Prep-work update:
  ❖ Hi, everyone. (Name) was the first to complete the pre-meeting assignment. Check out his comments at (location). If you haven't gotten to it yet, his post is likely to jump-start you.

- Welcome to the meeting! Thanks for the prep work you completed before this meeting. It helped me prepare, and as a result, this meeting will be focused and efficient.

- I am commited to keeping the prep-work relevant. Let me know if it ever seems more of a hindrance than a help.

- I'd like to acknowledge (members) for the high level of preparation for today's meeting. In particular, the fact that they (specific indicator of preparation) added clarity and efficiency to the meeting.

  - Who else noticed and appreciated a high level of preparation from a team member? Please speak up now or send me a comment via chat.

  - No—I wasn't fishing! But thanks for the compliment! Tell me what was helpful about that.

  - Our preparation affects the success of the team, and it's important for us to identify and acknowledge how we all did.

Perfect Phrases to Facilitate Virtual Team Meetings

There's a lot more to leading a virtual team than facilitating meetings, but being able to run an effective meeting is key. Here are some phrases to make your team meetings effective.

- Welcome! It's such a work of magic to get everyone together, so I thank you all for making this your priority and showing up! It's great to be together as a group. We'll make the best use of everyone's time.

Thanks for all the great input on the preagenda. We'll follow a revised agenda based on those comments. I have the current agenda posted on the screen, and you can follow along on the team site at (location).

First, let's remove distractions. We'll start off on mute, but unmuting is easy. I want you to be ready to participate.

Let's assign and review roles.
- (Name) will facilitate today's meeting.
- (Other name) will take notes and share them by (method).
- (Third name), will you please be our timekeeper? Let us know when we have two minutes left on a topic and when the allotted time is up.

The objectives of this meeting are (objectives). We'll lead with the topics that affect the most group members. At (point in the agenda), those of you who aren't involved in (subproject) can log off if you choose. Let us know so we can get closure with you before you go.

We'll start with five minutes of updates. I have a couple I'll share after (name) updates us on (item).

Let's review our metrics and celebrate our green items where we're meeting or exceeding our targets.

We've got some yellows and reds on the scorecard. (Name), as owner of (task), let's start with you. Update us on your progress and let us know what you need to get back on schedule.
- Who can support (name) with that?

Who has a win or an unplanned learning opportunity—otherwise known as a flub—to share?

- Our goals have shifted. Let's review what our targets are to make sure we're current.

- Okay, let's get back on track, we're on agenda item (number), and (person) just summarized (status). Let's look at (next topic) now.

- The scorecard is on the screen. Look at all that green! Let's spend a few minutes celebrating and sharing our achievements and learning.

- Next on the agenda is (topic). We need a decision about (item). Let's begin by defining the problem.
  - (Name), that's a topic for later. Let's keep our attention on (topic).

- It's time for our team scribe to summarize our action steps. This is how the steps will be posted, so make sure your steps sound like what you intend to do.

- In summary, here's what we accomplished and here are our next steps.

- Look for the meeting summary (in your e-mail/posted backstage on the site).

Perfect Phrases to Encourage Peer Feedback

The boundary manager and team leader roles are more facilitative than traditional management. It's not up to the leader to be the sole provider of feedback. If everyone comes to you with suggestions and challenges with each other, you'll find yourself in a hierarchical position that doesn't serve you or the team. Establish an environment in which people manage their own relationships.

Feedback isn't necessarily remedial. Feedback is information. Encourage peer feedback as idea sharing. Feedback can be about how someone can do a great job at something rather than just a good one.

❖ Virtual team feedback
  ❖ We posted a feedback survey to help us evaluate our team process. It includes individual member evaluations. There is a place for comments, so for any rating of less than a 5, please make a suggestion for how that team member could improve his or her contributions to the team dynamic and team success.

❖ Team assignment—stop, start, and continue feedback:
  ❖ Feedback isn't just for when things aren't working. The best alliances give feedback continually—fine tuning how they relate. If we wait until there is a problem to give feedback, we'll create resistance and miss learning opportunities.
  ❖ Over the next week, please give each team member feedback in the form of stop, start, and continue. If you can do it face-to-face or by video, that would be best. Phone can work too.
  ❖ Begin by requesting that your teammate stop doing one thing that he or she does that isn't helpful to you.
  ❖ Then, identify one other thing you would like for him or her to start doing that would be helpful.
  ❖ Conclude by noting one thing the teammate does that you would like him or her to continue doing.
  ❖ Come to the next meeting prepared to share a surprise, learning, or insight from the exercise.

❖ Virtual team member exercise:

> ❖ It's important to seek to understand and then to be understood, as Stephen Covey says. It's also important that the other person is satisfied that we understand what they have said. Let's each practice that over the next week.
>
> ❖ Pick a partner to practice feedback with. Say, "One thing that would help me is if you would _____," and fill it in with a useful behavior. Something like, "One thing that would help me is if you would acknowledge when and how you intend to act on my requests."
>
> ❖ If you're receiving feedback, respond by saying, "My understanding is that you're asking me to _____," and fill in the blank. Keep going until the person who started the ball rolling is satisfied.

● I received some feedback from the team that helped me recalibrate how I work with you. I learned that (point), and as a result I plan to (action). Let's go around the team and talk about how we each responded to peer feedback and made a change in how we did things.

● Remember, the purpose of feedback is to help the team succeed. If you need to unload, call me or someone else. If you have some useful suggestions, input, or operational requests, let your peers know as soon as you can.

● If you find yourself unable to communicate feedback effectively, I will help facilitate—but the first step is to offer it directly.

Perfect Phrases to Welcome New Team Members

Welcome and orient new members. Help them get up to speed as quickly as possible.

- Welcome! We begin new team member orientation by directing you to the public areas of our team site to get you familiar with our public persona. Soon, we'll provide passwords that give access to the general inside company information. Later we'll invite you into specific discussions that involve information that is proprietary to the team.

- Your home page is set to default to our new team member home page. It has all the information you'll need for the first 90 days.

- I want to schedule time with you to welcome you to the team and get you up to speed. I've got some appointment times for you to choose from. Let me know what works.

- We have a lively community on our network. They'll get you up and running in no time. Post your questions freely.

- I'm looking forward to our scheduled conversation. Between now and then, please review the team site to get familiar with who we are and how we operate. Don't worry—I won't be testing you.

- Welcome! I'm so glad you're on the team because (reason). (Example: I heard great things about your work on other teams.)

Let's start with the history of the team. Understanding how we got here always helps us understand where we are.

Here's a summary of our guidelines, processes, and procedures. You can find them documented on the team site, but I'll give you a quick overview with examples of what it looks like in real life.

Can you support those guidelines and processes? Is there anything that troubles you about them?

Check out our protocols for e-mail and other communication. They've evolved over time, so we don't expect you to master them immediately. We'll steer you if you misinterpret or forget any of them.

I'm the boundary manager. So let me explain what the boundaries are! If you find yourself spending time with or struggling with anything outside those boundaries, let me know so I can run interference. If there's anything in the team structure that interferes with your ability to do your job, I'd like to hear about that, too.

● Now, a brief introduction to the team members. I'll give you a quick picture of how skilled a group we are!

Next, let me give you an update of our progress on the project so far. We'll look at the key timelines and how we're doing.

What questions do you have for me?

● What would you like the team to know about you when we introduce you?

Let me go over the teleconference/videoconference protocols and etiquette. Don't worry too much about stepping on toes—I'll message you if you unwittingly cross a boundary. It's a forgiving group.

● Okay—I think we're ready to introduce you to the team at our next meeting. Thanks! This has been great!

Perfect Phrases to Introduce New Team Members and Encourage Inclusion

Help integrate new members as quickly as possible and encourage new member inclusion.

● (To team) (Name) is our newest member. I'll introduce her at our next meeting. In advance, please review her profile page on our team site.

● (To team) The first order of business is to welcome our newest team member. I've had the opportunity to speak with her, and here are a few skills, experiences, and personal qualities that stood out for me.

● (Name) was brought in because of her skill in (area) to (role). Let's go through each of our roles and talk about how her membership will affect what we do and how we can interface to use her talents most effectively.

  ● For example, what distribution lists does she need to be added to as a direct recipient? Which ones does she need to be added to as an informed recipient?

  ● We added her name to our task and role matrix. We'll start by looking at her row on the matrix, and then we'll see how her roles and responsibilities change the rest of ours.

- To help you get to know (name), I've assembled a short slide presentation from photos he sent me and other sources. So sit back for a couple of minutes and enjoy the show!

- I'd like each one of us to take a step this week with the direct purpose of integrating (name) into the team. Ask yourself, if I were in (name's) shoes, what would I need from me? And do it.

- (Name) is the latest member of this team. His résumé is available (where).

- Our team has changed so much and so often that sometimes even I don't know who's on the team. To get us all up to speed, I'll start by introducing our new team members and then we'll all introduce ourselves and our role.

- I just heard a term that some of our newer members might not be familiar with. Anyone need clarification?

- (Team member) is new at working remotely. I'd like each of us to do one thing to help her prepare for the transition.

- (Name), now that you're working remotely, what are your core availability hours?

- (Name), let's talk about what's different since you moved to a (home/satellite) office. Are there any challenges or concerns for us to manage now?

- We asked (new member) to take the (DiSC/SpeakStrong communication survey at www.speakstrong.com/inventory) that we all took. When he's done that we'll post his scores.

CHAPTER 11

Develop Adaptive and Collaborative Excellence

While some virtual teams are predictive, applying a previously mastered approach to a similar type of problem, the increasing majority are adaptive. They're tasked with accomplishing something new, and they develop the steps as they proceed.

If you hired well for an adaptive virtual team, this section will be easy for you. You might have some resisters here and there, but your job will be more a matter of opening a few doors than dragging someone kicking and screaming. Whatever your existing team agility level, adaptiveness is a skill that you can develop.

Perfect Phrases to Introduce Working Adaptively

The concept of adaptability or agility is new for many. People have been trained to look for precedents and sometimes apply old solutions to new challenges—like a Procrustean bed, where the sleeper is stretched or sliced to fit the bed, rather than the bed fitting the needs of the user. These phrases introduce what it means to work adaptively.

- Let's look at our adaptive experience levels.
  - Whose prior experience is typically with an adaptive, creative, flexible, dynamic, agile team?
  - Who's new to this way of working?

- Agility requires us to test new ideas in their early development with pilot conferences, where we share what we have so far and exchange ideas early.

- The team faces new challenges, and this will require us to adopt new approaches. We won't discard history or precedent automatically. We'll adopt new solutions as the situation calls for it.

- When Einstein observed that we can't solve problems with the same type of thinking that created them, I think he was envisioning virtual teams. Our biggest challenge will be to think beyond our old mindsets.

- If all we had were known challenges, we could plan each step. We could have static policies, stable information bases, and fixed procedures that would allow us to move forward linearly, executing a predetermined plan. Our challenge is greater than that. The challenges we face are new, and so the solutions need to be new too.
  - (Name), talk about what's different and new about this project for you and how you adapt.

- (Name), where have you had to discard old information or approaches and do things in a new way?
- Welcome to the world of working adaptively. Sometimes the problems we're asked to address are so complex or unfamiliar, we're not even sure what questions to ask.
  - Anyone else feel that way?
  - Let's just start asking questions until we start to get a sense of where we need to put our feet first.
- Here's what's different in an adaptive environment. The work is always changing. The problems we tackle are new. What worked before doesn't work anymore. And the solutions are generally unique to each situation.
- It takes courage to work in an adaptive environment, because the risks are higher. So are the rewards.
- Working adaptively means thinking in stereo. We need to note the patterns from the balcony, where we can see the whole field—and see the detail of the playing field at the same time.
- The very reason we have this team is because the vision and mission are complex and require innovation and information sharing.
- We need to look for openings, not closure. I understand that (idea) won't work as suggested here. Instead of shooting it down, let's see where it can lead us.
  - What obstacles lead us to believe that idea won't work?
- No one of us can have all the answers, and not even all of us can have all the answers yet. We'll need to look for answers as we go along.

- It's a challenge to resist the temptation of going for the quick answer. You know why we have to? Because there aren't any. We actually don't have a choice here.

- Working adaptively means being willing to stand in uncertainty until certainty reveals itself. So I ask you to have the patience to wait to jump into action until we find the best approach.
  - Is that the best approach, or are we considering it because we want a quick answer?

Perfect Phrases to Encourage Emergent Leadership

It's a delight to watch the dance of a leaderless team that is actually leader-full. There's an ebb and flow where people move forward and step back according to how the pull of the work aligns with the strengths of team members. If team members have a static idea of what leadership is, they might hesitate to step in when the situation invites them, fearful of overstepping their boundaries. These phrases will help establish an understanding of what shared leadership can look like.

- I'd like us to go through an evolution from leader-led to leader-prompted to fully leader-full.
  - In the first stage, the team will typically look to me for direction.
  - The second phase is more fluid—I'd like to see you jump in and lead where you believe you can make

the best contribution. If that is not happening, I will prompt you.

● In the final phase, it is a full-on high-performing dynamic and agile team where each person knows when to move forward and lead and also knows when to follow.

Think of me as a GPS system. I can give you insight into where different choices might lead. You're driving the car. You're in charge. You lead your own area.

Leadership means stepping forward when the situation calls for it and stepping back when the situation calls for someone else's expertise. Who would like to take the lead for (task)?

We could pick a leader for each task, but often the natural leader emerges when we get into the task. It seems we don't have a natural leader for this task, so I'd like to float it for a while and see who seems to fit naturally.

I'd rather have someone close to the action take the lead here.

In virtual teams, multiple leadership is the norm. It seems to me this (project/task) has your name on it, (name), because of your expertise. Do you agree?

This isn't a leaderless team—it's a leader-full one.

I'm your boundary manager. I create an environment where you can lead effectively without interference. I'm the lead on this when it comes to working *on* the system, but not *in* the system. That needs to be one of you.

Perfect Phrases for Improvement Kata Coaching Cycles

This phrase section defines a specific practice, or kata, adapted from those presented by author Mike Rother in *Toyota Kata*. Apply these phrases in sequence at regular and frequent intervals, even daily. This process is neutral—the questions are appropriate for any situation—and it works uniformly as a learning and continuous improvement tool in striving for new levels of performance rather than just remedially solving performance problems. The opening phrases in this section establish the practice. The subsequent phrases are my adaptation of Rother's five *Toyota Kata* questions.

- I'm not here to direct your work, I'm here to guide your learning process as you face the challenge you've been tasked with. Since this is an adaptive challenge rather than a set process that involves applying existing solutions, my role as boundary manager and team leader is to help you learn.

- I have a set of five questions that unleash creative skills to focus on the present task. They comprise an improvement practice similar to the one Toyota uses for continuous improvement.

- The questions are a road map to keep the learner focused on the objective while iteratively exploring ways to break through obstacles—via experiment, observation, and adaptation to unfolding events.

- Can we proceed with those questions?

- What's your objective?
  - What do you want the outcome/process to look like?
  - How do you define success?
  - How is it measured?
  - Where are you now? Describe your current status.
  - What obstacles stand between you and your target?
  - Which obstacle will you address next?

  What's your next step?
- When can we see what you learned from taking that step?

  That's it! We'll do this all over again when we meet. See you in cyberspace then.

Perfect Phrases to Coach for Self-Efficacy

Master coaches teach others how to learn. Adaptive coaching focuses on self-efficacy, or improving the team member's ability to solve problems, find answers, and learn new skills effectively. Coach to remove obstacles that keep the team member mentee from clearly seeing possibilities. Keep the path clear so learners can find their own way. Here are a few questions you can use.

Let's see if you can solve that (answer that) yourself.
- What's your target outcome?

I could tell you what I might try, but I'm much more interested in finding out what you need to know to decide for yourself. It might take a bit longer, but ultimately it works a lot better.
- Are you willing to take the longer path if it empowers you to work adaptively?

- As your boundary manager, my job is to clear the path for you to operate effectively. Rather than have me find your answer, let's see if we can quickly increase your competency (teach you a new skill) to solve this yourself. I'll help clarify what's in your way and find ways to approach the obstacles.

  If I ever forget my role and seem intrusive, please tell me.

- How do you define success?

  How does that align with the team goal statement?

  Is that your own definition or one you got from someone else?

  Is that sincere?

  - Why is that important to you?

    I noticed you got energized when you talked about (specific). Why is that?

- How do you measure success?

  - Does that accurately reflect your definition of success?

  - Is it possible to achieve those measures and not actually succeed in your definition?

- Describe what you were working on when you got stuck and what approaches might help you move forward.

  Give me metrics or concrete representations of that.

- How do you track progress?

- What's your current problem statement?

- What gaps are there between where you are and where you want to be?

- What stands in the way of your being able to do what you want here? What are your obstacles?

  How can you remove or address that obstacle?

  Are you describing an obstacle or a reason not to do it?

What information do you need to move forward?
- Where can you find that information?
- Who can help you get the information you need?
- As boundary manager, how can I help make that information available to you?

What are your top priorities?
- Does it matter where you start?
- Might it just be better to start somewhere?

How will you work with the team on this?
- Who needs to know about it?
- Who will you ask for input?
- Who do you need support from?

What processes and tools do you plan to use?
- Do you need any training or resources to do that?

Are you trying to plan the whole process here and now?
Could you start with a smaller step to see what happens and then decide a next step?

What alternatives have you considered?

What would that option cost?

What can I do to support you?

What might you learn from trying that?

What if it doesn't go as well as you hope?
- What's the best that could happen?
- What's the worst that could happen?
- Is the best that could happen worth risking the worst?
- Could you live with the worst if it happened?

When would you like to meet to talk about what you learn?

Perfect Phrases to Develop Continuous Improvement Thinking

The continuous improvement movement incorporates practices to cultivate improvement from "everyone, every day." In a continuous improvement culture, "human resources" means what it says. It refers to a deep valuation of employees as a company's most precious resource, and a resource the company invests in. That means a leader or manager will opt for a learning experience over a quick fix.

- I work from the relentless expectation of continuous improvement—the belief that it's both possible and important to improve any product or process.
  - That value is balanced with, "Have we met our goals adequately?" Don't be shy about pointing out if I mix these two goals up.

- I coach for continuous improvement. That means no matter how good we are or I am, the system/process/team dynamic is always up for improvement. As a tip—it's often easier to make improvement recommendations for good work than bad. With subpar work, it can be hard to know where to start! So if we don't accept something at face value, that doesn't imply it's wrong or poor work.

- I'm interested in what you accomplished, and I'm even more interested in what you learned from accomplishing it. That includes what you tried that didn't work as you imagined it might. Tell me about the false starts as well as the success you achieved.

On the surface, this seems like a failed attempt. That said, scientists always learn more from surprising results than from getting exactly what they expected. What did you learn that will help you in future endeavors?

Extraordinary performers give their work their all, despite who is watching. We picked extraordinary self-motivated people to be on this team. Why do people give discretionary effort instead of just sliding by?

● Why do you? Let's go around and talk about our motivators.

The smallest unit of any continuous improvement or learning organization is one. One person or one idea. One team member committed completely to learning from everyone and every experience every day will help us all succeed. If all of us have that commitment, we'll advance exponentially.

Let's go around and share what we each learned last week.

Before you share what you accomplished, tell me what you learned and how you went about learning it.

When you tell us how you solved the problem, please tell us what you tried that didn't work as well as what did.

I like the way you built on (something that happened previously). You learned from experience and took it one step further.

How did you go about finding a solution to the challenge?

Perfect Phrases to Introduce Dynamic Learning

Adaptive and dynamic teams exchange ideas freely and quickly. They practice what product development circles call *rapid prototyping*. One team member's idea might trigger an idea in another member that leads to a new approach.

In their *Manifesto for Agile Software Development*, authors Kent Beck et al. describe their iterative process this way: "We are uncovering better ways of developing software by doing it and helping others do it." It's about learning by doing. Iterative learning involves creating prototypes and revising them continually. Here are some phrases to introduce iterative learning.

- Think of the work we're doing and the team relationships as modeling clay. There's always an existing structure, and the next improvement helps to refine and improve its shape.

- We have to be smarter than a collocated team. And we do that by sharing ideas freely and often—by thinking together about what we're doing and how we're doing it. Every observation needs to integrate the latest team iteration and to think beyond it—take it to the next iteration. We're not negating each other when we add to ideas.

- Every shared interaction we have combines into mental models. When we share and combine our mental models and test them with each other, we think of better ones. That doesn't mean the old one was wrong, it means we've outgrown it—even if the oldest mental model was born 10 minutes ago.

- So here's where I'm taking your idea.

- Team formation is more of an iterative process than a linear one. We develop through many prototyping cycles. We take form in one area and then another, and the forms we create in the second areas will affect the form we started with. That's iterative learning and growth and development. It's not formless at all—it's dynamic.

- I know where we're going, and I know where we are. Every step we take will be a learning and discovery process that will allow us to see a little farther down the path. That's as far as anyone can predict.

- Be honest about how far ahead we can see and what we don't know. Admit when we've reached the limits of our knowledge and are starting to project and speculate.

Perfect Phrases to Encourage Collaboration and Collaborative Competition

Competition works well for simple endeavors where the options are clear—but the complexity of our cultures changes the nature of success factors. In complex systems where the options are less clear, cooperation has value, but collaborators win. That's collaborative competition, or *collabortition*. Collaboration skills are quickly becoming the hallmark of competitive ability. Collaborative competition uses the competitive urge to inspire team members to be the best collaborators.

- Teams are about collaboration. If you must compete, compete to be the best collaborator. Collaborators win.
  - So (name) gets today's collaboration recognition for (contribution).
- When it comes to virtual teams, the smartest collaborator is also the strongest competitor. Collaborative competition is kind of a "tough cooperation."

  That comment sounded like a rebuttal rather than a shared new perspective. How could you reword that so we build on each other's understandings?

  We're floating ideas for contributions, not refutation. Who can tell me the difference?
  - Contributions might note a flaw, but they redirect toward a higher iteration rather than tear down.
- Sharing information is the lifeblood of virtual team success. The minute one of us competes by putting our own interests ahead of the team purpose, that's the minute we lose our synergy and effectiveness.
  - Let's talk about how competition and power struggles show up on teams. What kinds of behaviors signal competition among people who should be cooperating?
  - In what ways is it happening here?

  Cooperation is useful, but it's nothing compared to collaboration. We need to come up with ideas none of us could have come up with on our own.

  I expect you think you're contributing when you comply without question. We didn't bring you on the team to go along with ideas that you know won't work without a challenge.

- Challenge my thinking here. Collaboration isn't about being party-manners nice. It's about being willing to offer an opinion, incorporate others' ideas, and build one iteration after another. How would you improve on what I just said?

- We're growing out of our hero mentality into an improvement-through-teamwork mindset. I see some ball hogging. That's not going to score more points for the team.

- No one gets commission on a sale that is never made, so get back on the same team! We rise and fall together—like it or not.

Perfect Phrases to Boost Strategic Use of Networks and Collaborative Technology

Many successful professionals attribute their achievements to strategic use of collaborative technology and teaming networks. Functional knowledge is the beginning of using collaborative apps and software. Strategic knowledge takes the tools to their next level where they can more than make up for the lack of face-to-face relating. Please read that last sentence again. It's true. They really can.

❖ Strategic use of our team and company networks:
   ❖ How are you using the team and company networks in ways that further the team and your own role as team champion? Here are some guidelines to help you make strategic use of the resources available to us as a team.

❖ Before you post, ask—who would benefit from this information? Is it relevant just to the team, or to the company as a whole?

❖ Post up the chain for a broader audience. If something you post will benefit the larger networks, post to those and include a link on our team discussion.

❖ Sharing good relevant information that positions you as an expert to a broader audience builds your personal brand and our team brand too. Plus, the broader the audience, the more hits you will receive and the stronger your participation metrics will be. Remember—post to the highest relevant network and notify the team and/ or individuals who will benefit from the information.

❖ The more people you're connected to in the organization, the more effective you can be. The more people we're connected to as a team through our members, the more effective we can be as a team.

❖ Please be sure to use the team name/logo/brand in all posts related to team activities.

● Once we develop our use of our team chat feeds (example: instant messaging, team Chatter, etc.), we can be in meetings and get answers back to the customer in minutes, where at one time it would have taken us days.

● (Subgroup) owns the buzz for the network this week.

● Tell us how you used the network strategically this week.

● Our top connector to date is (name). Way to team!

● The team/company networks are a great opportunity for you to show off what you know about (topic) so everyone can see—and learn.

● It shouldn't take any of us 20 minutes to find the information we're looking for, and then discover it's outdated.
In addition to properly annotating his own information,
(name of champion) has a practice of annotating documents he accesses for easier retrieval for the rest of us.
Let's support his efforts and do that too.

Perfect Phrases to Spark Synergy and Increase Reliance on Shared Intelligence

Synergy is combined action or functioning. It gives a feeling of
frictionless flow, dynamic inspiration, and continuous creativity.
The whole becomes far greater than the sum of its parts. It's
easier to describe what blocks synergy than what creates it. But
synergy is what makes teams—virtual or otherwise—so powerful and effective.

● Let's make transparency within the team our goal. We
have (a shared file system, intranet resources, etc.) to help
us do that. Please use these.

● Let's distinguish between "draft" and "completed staff
work" and discuss the role of each.
  ● Sometimes we need to see a draft, and other times
  we don't. It depends on the work and the roles. Don't
  withhold information, and also, don't flood each other.
  When in doubt about whether to share or not, inquire.
  Often findings that don't seem conclusive or relevant
  are useful to other team members.

- We'll monitor the contributions to our (knowledge transfer system/team site library). That means you aren't just asked to use the intranet—you're expected to. We'll also monitor and recognize those whose postings get the most hits, links, and mentions.

- Instead of sending me information with e-mail attachments, please post the attachments to the intranet. That way the information will be readily available to the entire team. When I receive attachments, I won't open them, but when I see links, I will.

- We're posting our contracts to the server to speed up the process. We all have access to each other's contracts now. That facilitates information sharing.

- I'd like each of us to talk about synergy. What is it?
  - When have you experienced synergy? What created it?
  - What has happened to block it?

- I love it when synergy happens. It's not something we can create deliberately, but it is something that we can provide a foundation for.
  - What creates a foundation for synergy?

- I honestly believe that all of us are more insightful than any one of us. That's why I'd like your input on (challenge or topic).

- Last week I was going to (example: postpone responding to a post), but I realized that would block the synergy. I didn't want to stand in the way of anyone's momentum.
  - What examples do you have of choices you have made in order to keep the synergy going?

● I've discovered that translating complaints into requests helps the synergy. Can we reword the challenge we're facing in terms of what we're moving toward?

● This idea is a seed. It's challenging to see the oak tree in the seed—but I think each team member can see a different aspect of what the oak might look like. Let's water the seed instead of complaining about it not being a tree yet.

● (Name), that was a great contribution to the team dynamic.

● Let's take our phones off mute for the next few minutes just to make it easier to respond dynamically—and see what kind of synergy it creates.

● How has the information flow been since our last meeting? Is there anything we need to do to keep it moving and the synergy going?

● To keep the team synergy going, please remove any distractions or temptations to multitask. Let's be completely present. If you find yourself tempted to multitask, ask yourself why, and explore what you would need in order to be fully engaged. It might be a signal that you're not really needed on the team—or at least at these meetings. If you're here, we want you here all the way.

Perfect Phrases to Explore Best Practices

None of us is as smart as all of us. Structure best-practice sharing into your virtual team. It will maximize performance and solve problems early on or even before they arise. Share best practices as a way to address issues. A great best practice is to have dedicated best-practice meetings.

- I'd like to share a best practice that worked well for me. (Example: Mary was experiencing some confusion discussing a document, and we realized we needed to annotate it better. When we added page and paragraph numbers, we knew right away what the other was talking about.)

- Before we review the information in the chart (name) made, I'll point out how clear the chart makes the information. This kind of visual communication is a great best practice.

- Who has a new best practice to share? Or an oldie but goodie that would be useful to the team?

- I love it when a subgroup sees a need and fills it. In this case, our (example: technology team created a team handbook with backgrounds and contributions for each team member) so (example: everyone would know whom to consult).

- Some of us have been fighting the good fight against e-mail overload and losing. Who has best practices you can recommend for that?

CHAPTER 12

Embrace Virtual Reality

As virtual worlds explode, collaborative software is becoming increasingly sophisticated and there are more tools that support virtual teaming than ever before. Many organizations have very sophisticated teamware. Even teams with no budget at all can create virtual places, have their own team feeds, have web conferences, and share documents online. Adapt the phrases in this section to the collaborative software and technology that your team uses.

Perfect Phrases to Encourage Pull Communication

The era of broadcast media was an era of push communication. The era of digital media is reversing that trend. It gives us all more choice than we ever had before in how we communicate and manage information.

One of the distinctions of well-functioning virtual teams is a high percentage of pull communication as opposed to push.

Distinguish between push and pull communication with your team, and move toward a pull communication model where quality information is available when team members need it. Pull is the language of the new virtual reality.

- Push, pull, what's the difference? It's the difference between having information forced on you and having it when you want it and are ready for it.
  - Push communication happens when messages are sent in ways that force the recipients to react as soon as they are aware of them. Unprioritized e-mail obligates the unfortunate receivers to wade through a sea of messages in their inbox to find the ones they want.
  - We can increase the pull of communication by prioritizing our e-mail.
  - An e-mail with no subject line is even worse. It says to the receiver, I'm too important to take the time to simplify your life by telling you what this e-mail is about. Again, that forces the receiver to open the e-mail to determine its immediate relevance.
  - We can increase the pull of our communication by using good subject lines with our agreed-upon priority codes.
  - Can you give some more examples of push communication?
- Pull communication is when the receivers access the information when they're ready for it. The web is pull communication. Information is sitting on the web waiting for you to be ready to access it.
  - Who's in charge with pull communication?

- Let's imagine a perfect world of pull communication where you only receive the exact information you need when you need it. When you're ready for some information, it's there waiting for you. Your inbox only has e-mails in it that you need. Every conversation you have is the exact one you need at that moment.
- It's a fantasy, but can you see how pull changes the dynamic? What would you say is the advantage of pull communication?
  - When might push communication be necessary?
- What category does spam fall into? Push or pull?
- Do you ever feel like you're spammed by colleagues and team members?
  - How can we define spam in a way that covers how we spam coworkers?
  - How can we keep from spamming each other?
- How can we use e-mail in a way that is more pull than push?
- There's more to push and pull communication than the modalities. Have you ever had someone try to "make" conversation? Sometimes the effort to force chitchat can actually interfere with real conversation happening. There's so much chatter going on that there's no room for casual interaction to bubble up.
  - Can you give other examples of push communication?
- Going from pushing information to making it available for pulling requires a change of habits. First of all, we need to agree to a medium we will check for urgent messages. Then we need to agree where to post and how to handle

important but not urgent information to make it available on an as-needed basis.

- It also puts more responsibility on the message sender to make sure the message has an attractor factor—that it's relevant, easy to access, applicable, and interesting.

- If we prioritize communication and availability, and if we exercise discipline in how we access information, we won't lose important and urgent communications that are mixed in with what amounts to spam.

  - So think in terms of pull when we communicate.

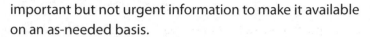

Perfect Phrases for Teleconferencing

These phrases are for team meetings, virtual coaching sessions, and other interactions that are conducted over the phone without a web or video component. They compensate for the limits of communicating in a solely audio format. Adapt them for communication that has a web component. Be clear about protocol in the beginning, and remember that people can only hear, not see. You'll find sample teleconference guidelines at www .speakstrong.com/teams.

- Here's our basic guideline for teleconferencing. Identify yourself as you begin to speak, and tell us if you need to go on mute, answer another call, or leave the room.

- Let's begin by introducing ourselves alphabetically and make sure we can hear each other.

- For those of you who are off-site, we made name tents with your pictures around the table. It's almost like you're here!

If any of you have background noise while listening, please mute yourself by pressing (instruction). You can unmute yourself by pressing (instruction).

When you speak, please preface your comment with your name so we'll all know who's speaking.

For the benefit of anyone who couldn't hear, that was (name) speaking.

That comment came from (name).

(Name), thanks for your input. (Name), what is your suggestion here?

(Name), are you shaking your head right now?

(Name), I can picture you smiling about that.

Since you can't see me, I'll tell you I'm really animated right now. My arms are waving trying to describe how big this feels to me.

I'm noticing some paper shuffling. Remember, we can't see you, but our sense of hearing is intensified.

We appear to be in agreement in our decision to (decision), but not everyone has voiced his or her consent. Rather than assuming silence is agreement, I'd like to hear from those who haven't expressed concerns or input into the decision.

(Name), I can't see you right now, but I assume you're nodding. Am I right?

Was that lack of laughter at my joke a technical glitch, or was it not funny? Don't answer that!

> ### Tip and Warning!
> ### Use the Technology Because It Adds,
> ### Not Because It's Cool
>
> Team members sometimes resist the latest and greatest technologies championed by technology enthusiasts because they've been burdened by learning features and applications that complicate their lives instead of simplifying them. Use technology because it adds to team effectiveness, not because it's "shiny" and can do interesting things.

Perfect Phrases for Web Conferencing and Videoconferencing

Web conferencing and videoconferencing add a visual component to the conversation. Use these phrases to optimize the value of your visuals, be they slides, graphics, or video images of team members.

- Please remember—we're on camera. We see everything you're doing. Not that we don't want you to scratch your nose when it itches, but this format actually highlights when you're distracted.

- Let's zoom our cameras in. We want to see everyone's whole face. Not quite that close!

- Let's do a quick check of all the technology we'll use during the meeting. A quick poll and voice check and switching screen owners. Now's your time to let me know if anything isn't working correctly.

Since we have the benefit of video, I'll start the ball rolling for us to use it to full potential. That's why I have a two-minute clip of (example: the CEO's presentation to the press about the project).

When a team member speaks, we'll put his or her profile picture on the screen. I've got all of our pictures up now for starters and a hello.

- Let's start at the top and say one or two things about our pictures. Some of us have cats', dogs', and children's pictures on our profiles, and I see a few superheroes too.

● (Name), please record the points to the whiteboard to help us all see what ideas are presented and what we're agreeing to.

● (Name), please write our decision on the whiteboard.
  - Okay—so is that what we agreed to?
  - Does seeing it on the board trigger any thoughts and ideas?

Simple PowerPoint presentations are great ways to present ideas to each other. They don't need to be polished—just combine words and visuals to make ideas simple and clear.

While you watch the presentation, text comments to each other reflecting your responses and impressions. We'll debrief them later.

● We have a mix of team members in the room and remote team members today. We want to do everything we can to include the remote team members. That's why each remote member is teamed with a group here in the room. If you're off-site, you're tasked with facilitation or note-taking during our small group discussion. We want you to have an active role so we don't lose you in virtual reality.

● I'd like each location to pull away from your computers for a few minutes and come up with three examples of what we just identified.

● This conference will be recorded for later viewing. You can find it (place).

Perfect Phrases to Optimize Collaboration and Shared Workspace Technology

There is so much new about virtual work and virtual teams that many competent professionals don't know how to maximize the opportunities. From using video and polling on web conferences to updating projects on project management software to encouraging active dialogue on discussions, adopting new technology can take some nudging and phrasing.

● We'll monitor the contributions to our knowledge transfer system. You're expected to contribute and will be rewarded for authoring popular postings.

● In reviewing the stats for this week, we see the top influencer for our team info-sharing network is (name). His discussions received (number) comments, and his documents received (number) hits. Way to go (name)! (Name) has become the one to beat for our collaborative excellence competitions.

Please send out an invitation to (event) so we can easily add it to our calendars and receive automatic reminders.

Our team meeting schedule is published online. Keep your availability times current so we can select meeting times that will fit your schedule. You will all receive notices when it is updated.

We created an online poll to get feedback on (initiative, decision, etc.). You can see how people are voting once you complete your poll.

We're creating a podcast about our progress and findings to share with our stakeholders.

There's a discussion happening on (team website) that needs input. Your insight in (subject) will help shape the discussion.

To avoid overriding each other's work, we'll designate one file owner at a time. The software allows you to check a document out when you need it. Since our software doesn't provide tracking, we'll communicate who owns a document at any given point by (means).

We need to agree to a file-naming protocol. I recommend our default naming protocol be: project short name/task/year/month/day/initials. For example DDC-GoalsProgress_2011-0928-bk.

Putting the date before the initials has the benefit of allowing us to sort by document title and section, and at the same time collect all the versions chronologically. Since we need to sort our files by date, I recommend we use a protocol that allows for that.

- Some of us aren't using the "track changes" function effectively. That creates work-arounds for other team members. If you have any doubts or questions, we can get you a tutorial.

- We have created virtual places in our best effort to make substitutes for physical places. Think about the kinds of conversations you have with face-to-face team members and see how you can duplicate them online.

CHAPTER 13

Monitor Progress

How are you doing? The best performance reviews result in performance improvement. Monitor the process and the progress to stay on top of challenges and keep people working at their best.

Perfect Phrases for Team Alignment with Dynamic Dashboards

Team dashboards help align team member activities by displaying key performance indicators in a standard format. They display individual and team progress. Dynamic dashboards make individual performance easy to update, monitor, and coordinate. You can see a sample dashboard at www.speakstrong.com/teams.

❖ Team dashboards:
  ❖ We're setting up the team dashboards. We're using the following key performance indicators based on stakeholder input assessments, management concerns, and team member input. Please review the indicators and

let us know if there are personal metrics you'd like to be able to monitor that aren't included.

❖ Senior management will measure you on (metric). To help you to meet their performance expectations, your dashboard reflects the data they use to evaluate your individual performance.

❖ Throughout the life of our virtual team, we'll float team member evaluation surveys. Part of the assessment will be based on the indicators on the dashboards regarding whether you meet your commitments to these metrics individually. We'll review these metrics throughout the life of the team to help you correct slippages early.

❖ Team dashboard update:

   ❖ Our dashboards are final. To create consistency, we use the same metrics for the entire team.

   ❖ You can see how you're doing in the single user view and how we're doing as a team in the team view.

❖ Based on our sharing rules, you'll be able to see (your information and the information for your area).

● Looking at the team dashboard, let's start with the areas where we're in the green. (Name), way to go. Let's give a round of applause (touch pad beeps) for him.

   ● Now on to the yellows.

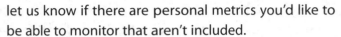

Perfect Phrases to Assess Team Process

There are three primary criteria for the success of a team: outcome, growth in capacity, and satisfaction. You want to achieve your goals, grow as a team, and have a positive team experience.

This section addresses team capacity. You can download a sample process assessment at www.speakstrong.com/teams.

- How do you think the team is doing?
- Let's go through the dynamics of effective teams and see how we're doing in each. Let's rate them on a scale of 1 to 10.
    - Did we clearly state our mission and goals?
    - Are the mission and goals clearly tied to objectives and tasks?
    - Are our team operating agreements clear, functional, and effective?
    - Do we operate creatively? Iteratively, building on each other's work?
    - Are our roles and responsibilities clear?
    - Do team members take the lead as the situation calls for?
    - How's our team trust level?
    - How safe is it to disagree and challenge ideas?
    - How well organized are we?
    - Do we build upon individual strengths?
    - How well do we support leadership and each other?
    - How well do we resolve disagreements?
    - Is our communication clear and open?
    - Do we make good decisions?
    - Do we cooperate well?
    - Do we collaborate well?
    - Do we pick up the ball for each other as needed?
    - Do we continually improve?
    - Are we communicating efficiently?
    - Are we sharing knowledge effectively?

- Are we contributing to the organization?
- Have we created a team people like being on?

Perfect Phrases to Assess Team Results

Of course, there's more to a successful team than having great processes and feeling good about it all. This section accesses team results.

- Let's go through our goals (or objectives) and see how we're doing with each.
- Let's begin by reviewing our plan versus actual progress. The accountability chart tells where we intended to be and where we are.
  - Where are we green—on target with our timeline?
  - Where are we yellow—behind?
  - Where are we red—in crisis?
- Are we satisfied with the team's progress?
  - Where are we doing well, and where do we need improvement?
- Let's review our stakeholder goals. How are we doing? How can we anticipate their assessment of us?
- Bottom line—are we getting results?

Perfect Phrases to Assess Team Member Leadership Contributions

"Leaders at all levels" is a requirement of industry today, and it is essential for virtual teams. Ask your team members to take

the free leadership development assessment at http://www
.speakstrong.com/leaderinventory/ (or one of your own choos-
ing) at team formation. Then have them take the assessment periodically to see if members are stepping up to lead when needed.

❖ Dynamic leadership assessment time:
  ❖ Please take the dynamic leadership assessment at http://
    www.speakstrong.com/leaderinventory/ and save your
    results. We'll discuss them at our next meeting.

❖ Kudos for (name) for having completed the dynamic leadership assessment already! That's leadership! Talk with
  you all about it (date of meeting).

● How did we do on the leadership assessment?
  ● Who has seen improvement in himself or herself?
  ● When you took it, who thought about how other team
    members lead in the different areas?
  ● Who is our role model of (leadership area from inventory)?

Perfect Phrases to Acknowledge Success and Contributions

It's easy to forget to acknowledge jobs well done, let people
know when their help made a difference, and celebrate accomplishments. In a virtual teaming world, it's actually very easy to
spread the word when someone does something that solved
a problem for you or otherwise moved the team toward success. If you can, get sponsors and higher-ups to put team members on a pedestal with a post when someone does something
remarkable.

❖ Note from (sponsor):
  ❖ Hats off to (name, photo attached) for a record week. (Name, picture attached) is a rock star with (achievement).

● Hi, everyone! I had to post to tell you I needed help with (challenge), and (name) showed me what to do. Thanks, (name).

● Here's a success story for us all. (Name) was in a meeting with (client) who asked if (example: our product integrated with their dashboards). He posted to the team network and got her an answer in two minutes with an upgrade recommendation he hadn't considered!

● Just so you know our team's effect goes way beyond the borders of this group, I want to let you know that (name's) white paper on (example: comparing service) has been downloaded (number) times, including by (recognizable person). There's a growing buzz about what we're up to!

● Team recognition: the buzz is spreading.
  ● I'm linking to an article in (local paper, significant blog, company newsletter) about our team. It's great to find that people are noticing our great work!

● Check out this report from (name, link). You'll see what he's been up to and get a few ideas of your own about knowledge sharing and best practices.

● Before we get into our agenda items, let's begin by celebrating the wins we've experienced this week/month.
  ● (Name) had a record week.
  ● I'll summarize the kudos that were posted to our team site.

- As a group we're (percentage) of our way toward our target and climbing!
- One thing that made a difference for our team was the way (name) did (contribution).
- (Name) was having a challenge getting an answer to the question of (question). (Name), tell us what you tried and how you connected with an expert who could answer that question for you.
- I'm checking our team discussion and see (name) has the most recent status update. Thanks for playing!

CHAPTER 14

Transform Obstacles

This section helps you address the inevitable blocks and challenges of virtual teaming.

Perfect Phrases to Restructure Team Operations

Don't blame or finger-point when a team member drops the ball. Consider it information to guide your next step. Explore the cause or breakdown from all perspectives, focusing on the desired results and the process rather than on personalities. If you have a people problem, focusing on the process will uncover it in the most effective way.

- We did some firefighting this week, and that tells me we're not operating optimally. Let's debrief what happened, what contributed to it, and how it could have been prevented. Then let's identify any improvements we want to make in how we work together.

We're behind enough that, frankly, we need to adapt or die. Let's refocus to get back on track.

The structure we have for collocated teams doesn't work for our virtual team. Let's look at our assumptions about teams and see where we need to change our mode of operations to adapt to being virtual.

I've noticed a time zone issue with (example: the document translation process). Is there someone in Asia who can take over (process) so the Asian team doesn't have to wait for the East Coasters to respond?

Has the team handbook been updated to reflect (change)? Who will correct it and post the changes?

We added team members and haven't lost any, and the team has gotten too large. Is there anyone who wonders if they might not actually belong on this team?

I'm hearing team members wonder what distant members are up to. That's my signal that we need a new level of coordination.

I suggest we move (names) from team members to advisory roles. Thoughts?

Let's review our communication process and see what is and isn't working. I notice some people don't follow our agreements to (example: check voice mail morning and evening). I'd like to find out why so we can know whether to adapt the agreement or encourage team members to follow protocol. Who is having trouble operating that way?

- (Name) is facing a killer deadline on another team and needs coverage. Who is up to speed on (skill or knowledge area) and can jump in?

Perfect Phrases to Address Mistakes

Scientists know that you stand to learn more from mistakes than from successes. That doesn't mean you should deliberately go out and make mistakes, but if people never make mistakes, they're playing it too safe. Address mistakes as what they are—gold mines of opportunities that can help teams move forward, if they have adaptive mindsets.

- Thanks for bringing this up so soon. I'd much rather deal with it now, when it's easy to fix.

- Let's start by looking at the process to see what contributed to the error.

- A mistake is a miss take. Think of it like a movie set. Cut! Now, let's prepare for the next take.

- What have you learned from what happened?

- Have you studied what led up to the error and what you might have done differently earlier in the process to keep the situation from exploding like it did?

- What's the key learning from this experience?

- Been there and done that! I don't like it when I make mistakes either. Now let's deal with it.

- Please share what happened with the team so we can all learn from what occurred. Your mistake could keep us all from making the same error.

- That miscalculation cost us time and money. I consider it an investment. To get a high return on that investment, let's replay it step-by-step so we can learn everything that experience has to teach us.

- It's not beating a dead horse, it's running an autopsy. We didn't get the response we were going for, and if we don't find out why, we'll repeat our errors.

- Failures are learning opportunities because they reveal limits in our system.

Perfect Phrases to Challenge Operating Agreement Slips and Noncompliance

Any system is as strong as the team's willingness and ability to use it. In the short run, overlooking operating agreement slips can seem efficient. In the longer run, efficiency requires taking the time to keep the system well oiled. Address breaches in team operating agreements as they arise.

- Operating agreements are easy to make up front and a challenge to enforce. Yet a single team member can undermine a potentially powerful system in the same way that one odd-shaped tire on a car would dramatically decrease travel speed. That's why I mention breaches as I find them, even if it might be easier to work around them.

Don't make me play the role of cop here. We made agreements, and I'm asking you to honor what you agreed to. I'd much rather be creating new ideas than enforcing simple agreements.

I won't be team cop. I need everyone to share the responsibility of reminding team members to follow our team operating agreements.

It might seem like I'm being hard here when I point out (slippage). I do it because the system only works if we use it.

If an agreement doesn't work for you, renegotiate it. Don't just blow it off. That feels like you're blowing the team off.

We agreed we would all monitor (example: text messages). That's not happening, so we send urgent messages through multiple mediums to make sure people get them. We need to honor our team operating agreements.

● If you send an e-mail without composing a relevant subject line (which includes the agreed-upon team coding) you create more work and confusion for the receiver. It's easy to forget—so let's remind each other.

Please remember to start a new subject line when you change the topic. It's too darn confusing to try to find information that's hiding out in a different e-mail stream. That's the protocol we agreed to, and it's the protocol we all need to follow.

I will respond when you post your message to the community info exchange. That way, everyone will see the question and everyone will see the answer.

- Please resend this with the agreed-upon (subject line, file name, etc.).

- Our naming protocol keeps our document libraries from becoming digital landfills.

Perfect Phrases to Address Technology Resistance and Competency Issues

Never assume team members' technological skill level. Unless you carefully hired for technological skills, some of the most brilliant team members might be functionally illiterate on basic collaborative technology. Technological illiterates share this with many who can't read: they often try to work around their limits rather than acknowledge them or get training. Use these phrases when technology resistance limits effectiveness.

- Technology evolves quickly, and it's impossible for any person to be versed in all that is out there. I don't expect you to understand every bell and whistle our software has. I'm more concerned with what you do when you face a technology challenge. If you don't know how to use a function the rest of us use, get help.

- How do you handle it when you need to do something and you don't understand how the function works?
  - Do you know how to Google specific error messages or other technology challenges?
  - Have you found tutorials on YouTube—where they walk you through the steps?

- Whom do you call?
- If your answer is that you do a work-around, you're not advancing your skills.

- (Name), I notice you don't respond to texts very often. Is it a preferential thing, or could you use some coaching in how to do it? We need you fully in the game.

- (Name), I've noticed that you (example: input document changes by notes in an e-mail rather than using track changes and comments).
  - We established our collaboration methods and adopted the collaborative tools we have for many reasons. If you need help in understanding how to use this tool/feature, here's a 10-minute online tutorial that will get you on track.
  - Or contact (name), who can give you some quick instructions. Please, don't just expect us to work around your work-arounds—it's inefficient.

- (Name), if you have difficulty getting the collaborative software to work as it should, please get help before implementing changes rather than doing work-arounds. The way you input ideas is confusing and puts a time burden on other team members.

- It's okay not to be up to speed on the technology the team uses…yet. It's not okay to stay that way when it interferes with performance. We have technology skills as part of the team member performance indicators because they're essential to efficient team functioning.

- It appears you're working around technological weaknesses. Work-arounds signal the need to upgrade skills.

Perfect Phrases to Address Underinvolvement and Inclusion Issues

Teams are like living organisms in many ways. They're dynamic systems where every part affects the whole. Those who are actively engaged both shape and respond to the changes in the team. Those who hold back can drag team effectiveness down. Address underinvolvement.

- (Name), we brought you on this team because of your expertise in (area). There have been many opportunities for your input that you haven't taken advantage of. We need your involvement.

- (Name), I notice you haven't contributed to the team discussion on (topic). With your expertise in (area), your input would be extremely valuable. What keeps you from contributing more?

- Some of the team members are contributing freely in the team discussions/on the team wiki. Others aren't, and I'm concerned there's some free riding going on.
  - Free riding undercuts the radical trust required for this kind of sharing. Please share your findings to add to each other's knowledge bases.

- I noticed you haven't been online/participated in the discussions. Is there something you need help with to be able to join in? We want to hear your voice.

- I see you haven't contributed to the team site. Do you need help in knowing how to do that, or are you having some technical difficulties with the site?

- (Name), your lack of involvement is leaving a hole in the fabric of the team.

- Hey guys, we're a team here. I know it's natural to meet informally with the people in your same location—but we need to include our virtual team members on relevant issues too. Post to the community info exchange so everyone can see the question and everyone can see the answer.

- I notice you haven't participated in meetings. Why not?
  - Do you want to officially be taken off the team?
  - Do you see a way you can contribute that we haven't tapped in to yet?

- We have experts on our distance team who can help us in different ways than our collocated members. If we don't use the community info exchange, we'll both limit our knowledge base, and we'll keep some team members out of the loop. We need to include everyone.

- To help us prepare for the meeting and use this time together effectively, some team members invested time preparing review documents. These were circulated before the meeting. It's clear by the lack of participation from several of our members in this discussion that many of you didn't review these documents in advance. Is that an accurate assessment?

- Not everyone logged in to the assignments. My question for the group is: what prevents us as individual team members from showing up prepared?
  - How can we remove those obstacles to help us all prepare and come to the meetings up to speed?

Perfect Phrases to Address Individual Performance Gaps

The best time to manage performance gaps is at the first sign, when the gaps are still small. Address any "yellows" (delays) at the first indication in your accountability tracking. The best way to manage performance gaps is to coach or support excellence before gaps occur. (See Chapter 11, "Develop Adaptive and Collaborative Excellence.")

- Team members can take their commitments to a virtual team less seriously than to a face-to-face or proximate one. It's tempting to blow off an assignment for associates on the other side of the globe when people sitting next to you think their work is more important. Is that happening here?

- It's tempting to hope someone else does the work for you while you're focused on proximate concerns. That's especially true if collocated workers write your performance reviews! I get that—and the team is counting on you to do what you agreed to.

- I want to check in with you, not to check up on you, on a regular basis. That way we can do any needed course corrections early. I see you're a little behind schedule on (task)—which isn't a major concern, but I want to make sure you're on top of it.

- Do you have any questions, concerns, complaints, comments, or anything else about the peer feedback you received?
  - Can I help you sort through and understand and then troubleshoot?

- I see your status on (task) is yellow. Let's troubleshoot it immediately, before it causes problems downstream.
  - What prevents you from being on target with that task?
  - Is there anything about the task that's unclear?
  - Do you need information in order to be able to complete the task?
  - Do you have the tools you need to complete the task?
  - Do you have the training to complete the task?
  - Are you aware of how the team depends on you to complete the task?

- When I lead from a distance, I need to respond to subtler nuances and gut concerns so I can catch problems when they are little problems rather than wait until they become big problems. I notice some things in your performance that I'd like to discuss now, mainly to be proactive.

- I'd rather empower you to get good results than try to force you. The bottom line is we need good results.

Perfect Phrases to Address Team Conflict

We define conflict as anything that damages team member effectiveness and undercuts team success. Many conflicts are avoided by honoring and updating team operating agreements, so check that section. Here are some phrases to address conflict.

- What did they say when you spoke with them about the issue?
  - Why haven't you raised it with them directly?

- Would you like some help with wording?
- Remember to focus on the process, not the person, and on understanding why they respond the way they do.

You don't have to love each other, but you can't withhold information from each other. You're still a team.

The team doesn't have time to indulge in blaming or offense taking. We've got to give it all to the results.

When you don't see the context someone works in, it's easy to expect a team member to always be available. We might not respect our distance team member commitments as we would if we saw them up close and personal. I see signs of unrealistic expectations among team members, so let's clarify availability agreements.

Conflict is normal, and the fact that it happens in no way implies team deficiency or team member flaws.

Conflict defines. It forces us to examine assumptions, ideas, and solutions. So if we think the fact that we have a conflict is a sign of failure, we're missing the opportunity we have for improvement right now. Let's look at the assumptions we're being asked to see.

Is this a system problem?
- Is the system getting in the way?
- Is everyone honoring the operating agreements?
- What prevents us from honoring the operating agreements?
- Do we need to change the operating agreements, redefine them, or apply them more consciously?

The second step in resolving team conflict is to put it in perspective with the purpose and the goals of our team.

Let's go around and review what that is. I'll start by reviewing the mission, vision, and goals we set for ourselves.

- There are as many sides to a story as there are people in it, and there is also a definition that incorporates all sides. We'll go around and define the problem from individual perspectives and then from a group perspective. So if one member thinks another member dominates meetings and the other member thinks the group doesn't allow enough time to report in, the group definition might be that we have competing time needs. (Name), please start this ball rolling by defining or describing the situation.
  - (Name), it's your turn.
  - Let's look at our individual definitions. What's the same with each? What's different?
  - Now let's work together to create a group description of the problem.

- Here's our group description of the challenge we face. Do we have consensus on that definition?

- Do we understand the problem? What else do we need to know before we explore solutions?

- Let's post ideas of steps we can take to resolve this conflict on the (virtual) whiteboard. Remember —no evaluation at this point—just ideas. There are no bad ideas because a bad idea could lead to a good idea.

- Let's review the whiteboard together and see what kind of alternatives we can come up with.

- We have several good ideas here. Which one should we try first? Please note that we're looking for consensus—which doesn't mean unanimous. And know that if we try something that doesn't work for you, it doesn't mean we're stuck with it. This is a learning opportunity for us all.

● Okay, we've agreed to try (example: a new e-mail subject code) to see what happens. To make sure we have consensus regarding this as a next step, remember, you don't need to think this is the best possible next step. You just need to not feel morally or ethically violated by it and be willing to actively support the decision.

● When shall we check back in to see what we've learned and what we want to stop, start, or continue next?

Perfect Phrases to Guide Strategic Technological and Protocol Work-Arounds

There are occasions where key contributors elect to remain technologically illiterate. The spirit of virtual teaming is always about getting the result. That will require occasional work-arounds. While we don't recommend tolerating a team member's refusal to spend a few minutes to learn to work in a format that saves hours of team member time, reality does demand occasional strategic work-arounds. If a brain surgeon has knowledge that will save a life, the team isn't about to decline it because it's not submitted in proper form. These phrases are for the *occasional* work-around.

● Let's face facts here. (Name) doesn't know how to use (technology) and isn't going to learn. We need (name) on our team and on board. How can we adapt to those limits so it doesn't undermine the system that works so nicely for the rest of us?

● Our partnering company set up a site for our joint project. Instead of all of us going to the site, remembering yet another password, and learning to navigate the site, let's designate two team messengers and spokespersons to post to the collaboration site and download info for discussion at our internal meetings.

● One of the senior team members hasn't followed some of the navigation that needs review. I suggest we set up a private meeting to review what was important from his perspective.

● We've got 20 authors on this project, and they use a variety of authoring systems. Even a small learning curve could be a deal-breaker for some one-time contributors. And just one person not participating in a system can turn into a nightmare for us—hours of our time spent reconciling concurrent edits.

  ● While collaborative software would be great, I think we're better off just requiring that people use track changes and letting them know that if we don't hear from them by the deadline we'll assume they had no changes.

  ● Basically we'll keep the big picture in mind, try to foresee any potential problems, and accommodate when we need to. Agreed?

  ● Does this put an inordinate burden on any of the rest of the team?

Perfect Phrases to Invite External Mediation and Input for Unresolved Conflicts

If conflict can't be resolved at the team level, the team might "agree to disagree" to move the work forward. Sometimes, the team needs to acknowledge their inability to resolve their differences and refer the issue to stakeholders. This could be a subject matter expert or people in higher positions of authority, such as team sponsors.

- We worked hard to resolve this issue, but we are at an impasse. We need someone else to consider the areas of disagreement and to either render an opinion or make the decision for us. We could use your help on this.
  - Here is the question that needs answering (or the decision that needs to be made).
  - We've considered the following options and found each had its relative advantages and disadvantages.
  - We can agree on the following points...
  - However, we still disagree on these points.
  - Can you help us?

- We're at an impasse on an issue, but we agree that we admire and respect your knowledge in the area. Can you help lay out the issue for us and guide us to a decision?

- As a team, we've researched and discussed the decision of (example: which microprocessor to use). We've explored our options in good faith and still are at an impasse.
  - We've gone as far as we can efficiently go as a team.

- We agree that to continue to debate and delay the decision would be a waste of team time.
- We would like you to help us through this impasse.

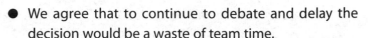

Perfect Phrases to Reestablish a Culture of Accountability and Trust

Trust is more easily maintained than restored, so watch for signs of slippage. When a team loses trust, it loses momentum. Members start second-guessing each other. The pleasure of and synergy from teaming is lost. Some of these phrases are directed at addressing trust issues at the very first sign of slippage.

- I know it seems like a small thing that you dropped the ball on (task). By itself it is, but the bigger issue is team trust. People need to know they can count on you, and slipups signal they can't.
- How can we know we can count on you for the big things when you drop the ball on the small things?
- Hey guys, I know it's natural to meet informally with the people in your same location—but we need to include our virtual team members on relevant issues too. The team needs to be able to trust that.
- We can do all the team-building activities in the world, but if someone is wondering if and when you'll return a call, he or she doesn't care whether you're a Harry Potter fan or what your favorite color is.
- Who owns this task?
  - What does that mean?

- Would you be willing to sign your name to your work for everyone to see?
- If you were another team member, swinging from a high wire needing to count on you to catch them, would you have the confidence to make the leap?

- We need to know that if any one of us is in trouble you'll let us know soon enough for us to deal with the situation. And if you aren't sure about something, you will let us know that you're giving us an opinion, not fact.

- For us to talk in depth about what happened isn't beating a dead horse. It's an important step in reestablishing trust.
  - Restoring trust starts when the person we counted on fully acknowledges the grievance of how he or she let others down in enough detail that the injured person feels heard and understood.
  - The next step is to sincerely apologize for the infraction.
  - Next is to state what behavior we intend to practice in the future.
  - Then, to help each other believe we'll walk our talk, state the steps that will reinforce that new behavior.
  - We've lost trust here, and we need to go through that process.

Perfect Phrases to Respond to Leadership Feedback and Admit Mistakes

Acknowledge feedback about your role as team leader and/or boundary manager. Let people know you understand what they're telling you and how you intend to adjust your course in response. A great way to encourage people to admit mistakes is to model that behavior. Be open about your own errors as team leader and as a team member.

- I'm hearing team members say they feel like their hands are tied. That tells me I might be controlling when I could be coordinating.
  - What specifically leaves you feeling like your hands are tied?
  - What would leave you feeling the flexibility you need to be effective while staying coordinated?
- When team members say they feel like they haven't been given much of a choice, it tells me I'm holding the reins too tight. My job is to keep us moving together toward our shared goals. If my attempts to do that stifle creativity, we need to talk.
- I need you to accept ownership and accountability. I don't want to hear you were just doing what I told you to do if things don't go as we anticipate.
- I understand we all create ways of doing things that work for us. I'm getting word that inconsistencies are causing problems. It's coordination time.
- I plan to be a fly on the wall in this discussion, not a fly in the ointment. If my input is too directive, let me know.
- I've heard the complaint that meetings are actually impeding our ability to get work done. We're always looking for balance. We'll cut back on our meetings.
- Am I mentoring or meddling?

- I realized I've been adapting the schedule to my needs unfairly. I suggest the next meeting be at a time that is best suited to our (location) contingency.

- I realize I created a lot of confusion by sending the wrong version of the document. I apologize—especially to (name), who spent a lot of time working with it. To avoid that happening again, I'll (example: check files before sending).

- I apologize for hitting "reply all" when the message was intended for a subgroup. (Subject of errant e-mail) isn't ready for general team input, and I'll let you know when it is.

- I'm committed to keeping you up-to-date on changes. I dropped the ball on one change. I'm sorry. I'll be more attentive in the future.

- I'd like to open by sharing a mistake I made and what I learned from it.

Close and Disband

When you reach the end of a project, you reach the end of a journey. When you close out a virtual teamwork endeavor, you close out a chapter of your life. Just as we insisted on a proper beginning for this journey, we encourage you to have a proper ending. Don't pretend it's just another "day in the life of." It's not.

Whether your virtual team continues past the life of your specific project or it disbands, take the time to reflect, celebrate, and honor yourselves for how far you've come. Then, shift from the past to the present and, from there, to a look ahead. Anything less undervalues what you've done and is a lost opportunity.

CHAPTER 15

Prepare for the End

As I wrote about virtual team completion, one book contributor Skyped to tell me she left a call early to devote time to reviewing the draft I had sent her. Ironically, the call she left early was the closing meeting of a virtual group she had been an active member of for a year. I reminded her of the importance of proper closings, and she rejoined her closing call. Funny how that works! It's too easy to skip over closings in favor of new beginnings and playing catch-up with neglected responsibilities. That's why closing requires clear direction from virtual team leaders.

Perfect Phrases to Champion a Proper Closing

Emphasize the importance of a proper closing to refocus those who have mentally left the team prematurely.

❖ Team (name) closing, celebration, and sendoff
  ❖ As we come to the end of our team journey, the last task ahead of us as a team is to close it out with clout.

Let's complete this last task with the same finesse we displayed as a team throughout the entire journey.

❖ We'll evaluate our effectiveness at the closing in the same way we evaluated our team effectiveness for all of our activities, so stay with us until the very end.

❖ To prepare for a dynamic conclusion to a powerful journey, please send pictures, documents, reflection, and other team memorabilia so that before we summarize what we have done, we can reflect on the journey we have taken together.

❖ Our last team task: debrief and closure

   ❖ Our final team task is to prepare for and come to closure.

   ❖ Team assessments are posted on our internal site at (location).

   ❖ Participation in the debriefing and closure event is mandatory. It's essential for every team member to prepare and attend to complete the team purpose of (purpose).

   ❖ Your participation will (will not) be a part of your performance evaluation.

● We're all experiencing the demands of tasks, relationships, and other priorities that have been neglected while we were intensely involved in the team. Still, let's stay present for and with each other until the virtual end, pun intended. We came in with a bang, and we want to go out with a bang, not a fizzle.

CHAPTER 16

Close Out the Virtual Team with Clout

Summarize the highs and the lows, agonies and ecstasies, side trails and successes. Think of it as a bit like soldiers swapping war stories as they return home victorious. They fought in the same war, but each has had his or her own experience. A simple slide presentation or video can bring memories to life whether the closing is face-to-face or virtual. Chances are team members will have forgotten much of the experience and will enjoy seeing just how far they've come.

- It all started on (date), when this team was a gleam in (originator's) eye. She went to (name) with the idea, who exclaimed, "How's that supposed to happen?" The rest is history. I like history! So let's share stories!

Before the team was formed, some of the ideas for the team name were (discarded names).

What's the funniest thing that happened on this journey?

Who thinks he or she might have made the biggest blunder? Will you share it?

What were we most naive about when we began?

What was your biggest surprise in the journey?

How did our experiences differ?

How are you changed by this experience?

What about this experience could you not have imagined?

Let's share some of our earlier versions of (team agreements, documents, etc.) to remind us how far we've come.

To symbolize where we started and where we are now, I have the following…

Perfect Phrases for Mutual Team Member Recognition

Have a recognition fest. This is like the journey review, but with shared acknowledgments of how collaborative input and other contributions made the difference.

We had a lot of adventures. Now let's talk about the heroes of our individual adventures. To start the ball rolling, I'll note a few heroes that emerged in our journey review.

- (Name) noted that a huge turning point came for her when (name) did (action) and said (words). What other individual hero moments do we each have?

- Who made a difference for you in this journey?
  - How did that affect you?
  - Why did that affect you so much?
- Who became an expert with earned authority for you?
- Who became your go-to person when you were stuck?
- Who really had your back?
- Who really got what it means to be on a team and gave themselves wholly to the team effort?
- Who got you to see things you might have missed?
- Who helped you break through just by listening?
- Who seemed to understand in a unique and useful way?
- It feels like we've grown through our participation on the team.
  - I'd like each one to share how you feel you've grown through your participation on this team.
  - Now let's share our observations about how team members have grown or developed—ways they've moved forward.
  - What are each of our next steps in our careers, jobs, or lives in general?

Perfect Phrases for Formal Recognition and Acknowledgment

If you recognized team member contributions and successes all along, providing recognition at the journey's end should be a simple matter of reviewing your posts, e-mails, team meeting agendas, and other notes. You can also prepare for closing by circulating a survey and presenting awards based on the aggregate data. The previous section gave spontaneous subjective recognition for support. This section provides acknowledgment based on data and records, and aggregate team data.

- Now it's time to acknowledge those whose contributions stood out as a whole. Our virtual teamwork Oscars.

- We couldn't have done this without the help of our sponsors. Here are some pivotal ways each sponsor supported the success of the team.

- (Name) broke all records by (achievement).

- (Name) reached new levels by (accomplishment).

- The award for most notable collaborator goes to (name).

- The award for the best troubleshooter goes to (name).

- The award for top community info exchange influencer goes to (name).

- The award for (marketing, communications, sales, customer service, product development, creativity, support, etc.) goes to (name).

- Now let's celebrate how we beat all records as a team by (achievement).

Perfect Phrases to Provide Team Recognition

Move from team member achievements and contributions to team accomplishments as a whole. Some areas of recognition will be external, others team-generated.

Here is the challenge we were faced with. (Identify challenge.)

We wondered how we would be able to accomplish that. Well—we surprised even ourselves.

Let's look at what was in our way. One of our biggest obstacles was (obstacle).

- To address that obstacle we (approach).
- Some of the things we learned about the obstacle that we hadn't realized were (discoveries).

We set our purpose as (purpose). Our goals were (goals). To achieve those goals we established a series of objectives. Let's go over them one by one and see how we did.

- We started at (metric) for (objective number one). Our target metric was (goal). Here's how we did. (Results.)
- We surpassed our target by (results).
- We didn't quite meet our targets in the areas of (area). (Explain.)
- Our targets were ambitious in the areas of (area), and although we fell short of our intended metric, we're proud of our achievement because (reason).

Some of the external recognition we received was (recognition).

We won the following awards.

The company as a whole achieved the following awards, (partially) due to the efforts of this team.

Some unexpected benefits of the team efforts are (examples).

Because of the work of this team, (end users) are now able to (ability).

Our functioning as a team improved dramatically. Some of the best practices we developed and embraced are (examples).

Our dynamic team assessments indicate an increase in team effectiveness and functioning. This was particularly evident in the areas of (areas).

Perfect Phrases to Debrief Lessons Learned

The phrases above are feel-good (not fluff) recognitions to celebrate team accomplishments. This section focuses on lessons learned to move forward, positive and negative.

How was your experience on the team overall?
- What worked for you?
- What didn't work?

In retrospect, how effective was the team setup?

Did the purpose statement provide a genuine guide and pull toward team results?

Were the goals clear and useful?

Did the achievement of goals accomplish the team mission?

In retrospect, how SMART were the SMART objectives?

How clear and useful was the role process and chart?

What do you see as the key team learning during the process? Knowing what you know now, what would you recommend the team do differently were we to start over at the beginning?

- What advice do you have for others forming virtual teams and working virtually based on your experience?
- Did the system support the team process, teamwork, and team results?
  - How?
  - How did the system interfere with the team process and effective team functioning?
- How effective was the community info sharing network for you?
  - What could have made it more useful?
  - What recommendations do you have for leadership, sponsors, and engaged stakeholders about best practices for supporting a team?
- What recommendations do you have for virtual team members who want to leverage teamwork for team results and for their personal success?

Conclusion

There's a saying that a man who wins a million-dollar lottery is a man with a million dollars, and a man who earns a million dollars is a millionaire. The implication is that riches come from the experience of earning more than from the million-dollar outcome. Virtual teamwork is much the same. Team members share in their lot even though some do more of the heavy lifting and others free ride at times. Performance management keeps the workload balanced to a degree, but life is never fair, and woe to the virtual team member who expects it will be.

Generally people see through free riders in the transparency of a virtual world, but whether they do or not, the true winners in any virtual team project are the ones who gave themselves completely to the outcome. There is something magical—almost transcendent—about immersing oneself in striving toward a common good—to an outcome that is greater than oneself. Those who do are the virtual team winners, and those who hold back miss out on rich and rewarding experiences.

The purpose of this book is to provide a practical and useful guide for virtual team players and managers. One measure of our success is in how it helps you, the reader, embrace and operate in a virtual world. Another measure is how transformative

and satisfying the writing process was for the authors and contributors. When anyone commits to a collaborative outcome,
the story behind the story will rock his or her world. Those who
walked closely with me on this book say it changed them as I
know it changed me. That's the power of collaboration.

We are here as collaborators for you. Let us know how we can
support your virtual experience. Let us know how we can help
you create your virtual dream team, navigate a virtual nightmare, or just figure out how to get your colleagues really on
board with your purpose.

In true virtual form, rather than listing all the referenced
resources, such as team assessments, in this book, we offer a complete, evolving list of downloadable forms at www.speakstrong
.com/teams. We'll be adding to the resources there, so check
them out. And thanks for playing. Without you, there would be
no book. Keep on aspiring!

About the Authors

Meryl Runion is a Certified Speaking Professional and the creator of the SpeakStrong Method of Communication. Her 10 books and keynote and training events provide PowerPhrases that help professionals say what they mean and mean what they say without being mean when they say it. Meryl's books have sold over 350,000 copies worldwide. She lives in Cascade, Colorado, where she collaborates with a robust virtual community of dynamic professionals, hikes, dances, and helps people figure out how to say things.

You can reach Meryl at

❖ MerylRunion@SpeakStrong.com

You can get her latest updates on virtual team forms, documents, and other resources at

❖ www.speakstrong.com/teams

Lynda McDermott is President of EquiPro International, Ltd., an international management consulting firm that specializes in leadership and team development, including virtual teams. She has worked in over 25 countries to launch and develop cross-functional and leadership teams for companies such as Pfizer,

Procter & Gamble, Hearst Magazines, PricewaterhouseCoopers, and sanofi Pharmaceuticals.

Lynda is coauthor of *World Class Teams* and is a Certified Speaking Professional. She is frequently called upon to present keynotes, workshops, and webinars for teams and team leaders, from the executive suite to the field force. Because of her extensive travel schedule, Lynda also "virtually teams" with her husband, Bill, to raise their teenage daughter, Carylyn.

You can contact Lynda at:

- ❖ E-mail: lmcdermott@equiproint.com
- ❖ Website: http://www.equiproint.com
- ❖ LinkedIn: http://www.linkedin.com/in/lyndamcdermott
- ❖ Twitter: lyndamcdermott